Altars
Made Easy

Illustrations by Claudia Karabaic Sargent

Altars
Made Easy

A Complete Guide to Creating Your Own Sacred Space

Peg Streep

HarperSanFrancisco

A Division of HarperCollins*Publishers*

HarperCollins Web Site: http://www.harpercollins.com
HarperCollins®, ☙ ®, and HarperSanFrancisco™ are trademarks
of HarperCollins Publishers Inc.

Book design by Martha Blegen

FIRST EDITION

Library of Congress Cataloging-in-Publication Data
Streep, Peg.
Altars made easy : a complete guide to creating your own sacred space / by Peg Streep.
Includes bibliographical references and index.
ISBN 0–06–251490–3 (pbk.)
1. Sacred space. 2. Altars. I. Title.
BL580.S77 1997
291.3'7—dc21   97–21926

99 00 01 ❖ RRDH 10 9 8 7 6

For Alexandra, shining light

Contents

Altars and Transformation   199

Altars
Made Easy

The Heart of Sacred Space

While I was writing this book, the question people asked me most often was, What *is* sacred space? Their next question, after hearing that the kind of sacred space I was writing about was *not* a church or a temple or a cathedral, was invariably, How do you make sacred space?

In fact, we can't "make" sacred space the way we "make" a cake from a cake mix. What has to come first is the recognition of and the need to connect to an order of being beyond the self, beyond the temporal world. We need first to allow the possibility of wonder and awe and enlightenment and to acknowledge our need for spiritual nourishment. We need, in short, to make room for the spiritual part of ourselves. Once we have done that, each of us will, in time, create an abundance of sacred space.

What *is* sacred space? It is a place where, as Joseph Campbell put it, wonder can be revealed. It can be found indoors and out, in homes and in offices.

The idea of sacred space is probably as old as humanity itself because the search for the spirit has *always* included the idea that the natural world is a book of signs and symbols of the divine, available to all who want to read them. The underlying idea of sacred space has remained the same, even though, from culture to culture, from one people to another, from century to century, the words of humanity's spiritual vocabulary may change. Sacred space is a physical place where the divine or the supernatural can be glimpsed or experienced, where we can get in touch with that which is larger than ourselves.

In our contemporary times, building altars—personal places of prayer, ritual, and meditation—is one way of acknowledging the sacredness of all the space we inhabit, from the macrocosm of the blue planet to the microcosm of the home, the office, and the garden. By acknowledging that something larger than ourselves with greater purpose exists, we create an environment where a sense of the sacred can be realized in the details of our everyday lives and in ourselves. Altars don't "make" space sacred; they work by showing us what has been there all along. They release energy within us and around us that we simply may not have been aware of. As part of a creative process, they help us refocus our spiritual eyesight. As Cloe Crawford Mifsud, who lectures on and leads tours to the sacred islands of Malta, explains it, the altars she has in her house are "visual clues when I'm caught up in daily life. They center me and bring me back." Or, as she puts it even more simply, "People on the earth plane need spirit."

For thousands of years, people have sought to bring the divine or the supernatural into human time and space by a simple act: the building of an altar. Then as now, an altar can be as simple or elaborate as its creator wishes. In the hands of the wealthy or, in days gone by, of queens and kings, altars were built of the most precious of woods—cedar and ebony, among them—and adorned with gold and silver, precious gems, and the finest of fabrics. In the hands of the humble, altars have been no less effective in enriching spiritual life when made of scraps of wood and simple bits of woven cloth and gifted with small offerings of fruits and meadow flowers.

I wrote this book to help you enrich the process of creating sacred space so that you can build altars that are meaningful and reflective of the spirit within you.

I've often been asked by people who are just learning about domestic sacred space what differentiates a grouping of objects—family photographs on a mantelpiece or table, a collection of ceramics or glassware, a gaggle of angels or gargoyles on a shelf—from an altar. For many people, the answer is, I think, intention. What may begin as a collection of loved and meaningful objects or mementos ends up being something quite different when the person taps into what the grouping means for him or her, what it articulates. If you take a look around your home, you are likely to find that, even without being conscious of it, you've organized the things you own not just by how they look but also by what they mean to you. Take a moment to think about it, and you will probably discover that certain objects or places in your home make you feel more comfortable or energetic or more in touch with yourself than others. Building an altar is the next step to awareness.

Creating altars will permit you to articulate feelings and thoughts in a physical way, bringing those feelings and thoughts into full consciousness. Yet, as a creative process, altar building draws on unconscious thoughts and associations as well, bringing thoughts and feelings we may not have been fully aware of out into the open. For example, Nancy Blair, an artist and writer, told me that, for her, the act of creating an altar is not as conscious as setting out to do an errand; it is *not* "Now I am going to make an altar for my kitchen." Building an altar lets us tap into what's really inside and shows it to us in a physical way. Sarah Teofanov, an artist and ritualist who teaches courses on altar building, remarks that we can learn from the process itself, for "what we choose *not* to put on our altars informs us as much as what we *do* place on them."

The very act of creating sacred space makes us spiritually receptive to the sacred, as well as giving us a physical place to pray or meditate or perform rituals. Tom, a musician, says simply that creating a shrine or altar gives you a place to find "what connects your heart to the larger heart." And, as he says, "Whatever does that for you is what works." Rob, a practicing Tibetan Buddhist and a software engineer, echoes that thought: "Connection is what makes a place sacred." In addition to his traditional Buddhist shrine, a private place, Rob has created a family shrine on top of an antique secretary in a prominent place in his apartment. Photographs of all the members of his family, including his two parents, who divorced when he was young, and a drawing of the house in which he was born grace this shrine; he is in the process of surrounding the family shrine with photographs of everyone who plays a role in his life. In his words, this shrine "helps to integrate my life," for it "acts as a reminder of the part of my life that is beyond me."

Humanity's first sacred spaces were not, properly speaking, altars at all, but places already known to be holy, where the presence of the supernatural or a deity was keenly felt, and where, as a result, rites and ceremonies took place. Many of these sacred places were on elevated peaks, near water and stands of trees, or deep in the earth, in caves and caverns. Building an altar or, later, a temple to house an image of a deity, did not make a place holy; the holiness of the space preceded the ritual gesture. More important, from ancient times through the early centuries of the common era, the distinctions between the sacred and the profane, the spiritual and the mundane, that are now part of the historical legacy of our Western culture did not exist. Landscape and space were holy because they manifested the divine spirit, a fact made concrete by the outdoor ceremonies and rites of ancient Greece and Rome; in the same way, indoor space—the hearth or the doorway—was sacred because it was emblematic of and belonged to a goddess or god. The idea that a building or edifice—a church or a temple—is needed to make a place holy is a much more recent idea.

Separating our "spiritual" identity from the other identities we have in our lives—as workers and professionals, as wives and mothers, husbands and fathers—is also, in the scheme of history, a recent event, and a Western one at that. In most parts of the world, the ritual offering of gifts to the gods and goddesses at home and at work, at personal and public altars and shrines, is part of everyday life. Even in our Western past, the progression of life and the act of making offerings were virtually inseparable. The ancient Greeks offered gifts to the gods and goddesses not only in thanks for survival and health but also to mark passages in their lives and to continuously rededicate themselves to the deities. Thus, children reaching adolescence offered up their childhood toys, while a woman delivered safely in childbirth might offer up the clothing she wore during her pregnancy. The practice of household worship was, in fact, so ingrained in the daily lives of succeeding generations of Greeks and Romans that, in 392, the Christian Emperor Theodosius forbade by law the private offerings of fire, incense, and wine.

Immigrants to the United States have often brought with them traditions that connect spirituality with everyday life, only to see the later, "Americanized" generations abandon these traditions. Many people I have spoken to recalled the saint's shrine in their great-aunt's yard or the altar to the Virgin Mary in their grandmother's or great-grandmother's living room. Gerard remembered that, every morning, his

Italian-born grandmother sat at the kitchen table—always in the same chair, which was her place at the table—and gathered together sacred objects, such as devotional images and objects, and her rosary. Each morning she would murmur words and sometimes perform small rituals—he remembers her putting droplets of oil into a small saucer of water—to assure her family's continued health. Unfortunately, the meaning of her ritual has been lost to her descendants. Another woman, now a grandmother herself, remembered *her* grandmother's elaborate Catholic shrine—with the Virgin Mary at the center and other saints surrounding—which sat in a place of honor in the dining room. Each morning, her grandmother would light candles and gift the shrine with flowers and food. The children were strictly forbidden to touch the gifts, for they assured the protection of the saints they honored.

Today, many of us are once more seeking out ways to integrate our spiritual lives with our "daily" ones, to acknowledge the spirit within us, and to celebrate and honor our own life passages through ceremonies and rituals, often conducted within our own homes, either alone or in the company of friends. Rediscovering the importance of sacred space in our lives can take many different forms, and throughout this book, I have tried to emphasize that there is no "right" way of creating sacred space or using it. Whereas in some spiritual traditions—Tibetan Buddhism, for example—the objects on an altar are prescribed, in many others, how sacred space is created is entirely up to the individual. Some domestic sacred spaces are used primarily for prayer or meditation and are set apart rather formally. Others, like those placed in every room by the Catholic mother of a friend, are simply beautiful images or angels; they are there to remind the occupants of the home of the power of prayer. In difficult times, they help everyone reflect and appreciate the role holiness plays in human life.

The word *altar* comes from the Latin for "high" and thus probably reveals the primacy of mountaintops as sacred space; technically, it describes a place where offerings or sacrifices are made. The word *shrine,* now a niche for sacred objects, once described a chest and, later on, a reliquary for the bones of saints. Throughout this book, I use the words *altar* and *shrine* interchangeably, although it could be argued that neither word quite fits the tremendously creative spiritual work many of the people described in these pages do.

The Language of Sacred Space

The Spirit of Sacred Space

On top of a small table in the living room of a garden apartment in a small Eastern city sits what appears to be a random collection of objects. The bottom layer is a beautifully woven yoga mat of many colors. On it are two photographs of men and one of a woman sitting in the lotus position, an incense burner, a small statue of an angel, a representation of the Indian elephant god Ganesh, and a portrait of a female saint. Lying among these are a strand of pearls and an unset carnelian.

Because Diane's shrine is in the living room of her apartment and can be seen by anyone who enters, it is deliberately unobtrusive, because she feels strongly that her spiritual space should not be imposed on anyone. And yet, as in all shrines and altars, every object she has assembled has both personal and spiritual meaning. The yoga mat was a gift from someone whose spiritual insight was valuable to Diane; the photographs portray gurus whose teachings were important, although she has long since left the ashram where they taught. The angel was given to her by a friend so that it might watch over Diane. Diane is a musician, and both the god Ganesh, traditionally the remover of obstacles, and Saint Cecilia, patron saint of music, connect to her profession and her greatest pleasure. The pearls and carnelian were chosen for their beauty and simplicity.

This small area is a place of quiet for Diane, where sometimes she sits and gathers as much energy and peace as she needs to live happily. Usually, when she meditates here, she adds to the altar's top a burning candle, a flower, or something beautiful that has caught her attention. She follows no particular rite, nor does she meditate at any specific time. The shrine is, as she says, simply a small oasis she visits when she needs to.

When men and women talk about their altars, regardless of their faiths and rituals, the same words come up in their descriptions. Some of them refer to the process of seeking the self: *energy, direction, meaning.* Still others address state of mind: *peacefulness, calm, strength.* Usually, too, there are words that connect to finding the sacred in daily life, focusing on something larger than the self and the day-to-day: *prayer, meditation, communication.* It becomes immediately clear that making an altar is not like decorating; it is a search for meaning or a *process* of discovering what has meaning for you.

Process is another word that pertains to the making of altars, for it reminds us that making an altar literally involves putting spirituality into physical form. It is an action that articulates an individual's spirit and energy, as well as his or her needs of spirit and energy. Many people describe their altars as providing important reminders of what they sometimes forget in the rush of the day-to-day: to remember to reflect, to remember to be true, to remember to live a dedicated life. Altars make us mindful.

Ann Evans, who trained at Union Theological Seminary and is now a ritualist dedicated to celebrating the divine feminine, has tried to make her entire home, not simply her altars, sacred space, for she feels it is her dedication to sacred space that allows the sacred to enter her life. As she puts it, "The Hebrew scriptural injunction to 'keep the Sabbath and make it holy' is so difficult in this secular world where distractions and responsibilities abound. I am gregarious and outgoing, and it is difficult for me to honor the silence and to see the rhythm of the day that allows us to appreciate the little miraculous moments." She finds that slowing down—being mindful and careful of her space, straightening and cleaning—brings the sacred in.

Energy is another important part of altar building. Many people build altars and choose their placement in the home to energize that space for a specific purpose. The altar one woman built for her home office deliberately omitted any reference to her children, because in this particular area of her life, the energy she needs cannot be deflected by other concerns. The altar provides the focus she needs. Marilyn Goldman places her altars in the rooms in which she spends the most time; they are deliberately highly visible. Marilyn began building altars after traveling throughout the Pacific Rim; she found herself drawn to the color and artifacts of the daily rituals at shrines that were part of everyone's daily life, particularly in Indonesia and Bali. Her altars are eclectic, with statues of deities and goddesses from many cultures along with personal objects, all things that have energy or personal resonance. Her altars, as she puts it, "acknowledge and remind me that there is a higher spirit."

Many people build specific altars to help them focus and clarify their thoughts and intentions, to gather up and strengthen their spiritual energies. Julie (Jess) Middleton builds altars to, as she says, "try to get my whole life to be part of the ritual dance." She built an altar specifically dedicated to friendship after receiving a telephone call from a formerly close woman friend from whom she had been estranged for over a year and who now lived thousands of miles away. The two women made a telephone date to talk at length, and Julie built an altar to help what she hoped would be a healing process for both of them. She began with a green cloth on the altar's surface to symbolize the close and shared connection to the natural world that had formed a basic part of the friendship. On top of the cloth, she placed a white triangular piece of lace, an emblem of the feminine and of softness. A statue of Kuan Yin, goddess of compassion, was placed on the altar to bring mutual compassion and understanding to their talk, as well as a heart-shaped candle and a pair of earrings the now-estranged friend had given Julie. Because both women are lunar, a moon goddess was added, and then an amethyst egg and a small piece of amber, "just because it wanted to be there." Candles were placed at opposite diagonal corners of the altar to signify the estrangement between the former friends. And, as the two women talked and healed, Julie moved the two prayer candles closer and closer together until they were joined.

Everything about an altar is ultimately personal. Though there are philosophies and systems of thought for guidance (*feng shui* or the Native American medicine wheel, for example) or traditional symbols (the *chakra,* or the cross, now associated with Christianity, among many others), there are really no hard-and-fast rules. The inspiration to build an altar may arise out of any number of circumstances. Maria, the neighbor of a friend and a practicing Roman Catholic, had a dream in which she built a shrine to Our Lady of Montserrat, a patron saint of her native Spain. The shrine now stands in the corner of her living room. Ed, a freelance writer who works at home and sometimes feels bombarded by communication from the outside world via phone and fax, simply felt he needed to carve out a place for reflection where no one would disturb him.

Personal shrines and altars are *not* churches, temples, or ashrams, for the latter are places of refuge set apart from the pressures, pains, and pleasures of daily life. Domestic altars are deliberately set into the everyday, as a way of imbuing the ordinary with the sacred.

My own primary altar is in my kitchen, set on a long window ledge above my stove and counter. The kitchen is the center of life in our house; it is the place where my daughter does her homework, where my family eats and the dog and cats are fed, where the newts and the tree frogs live in terraria, where I also sometimes work and write and always talk on the phone. Decidedly informal, it seems to have an energy and warmth all its own. When we have guests, regardless of the enticements I have left out in our comfortable living room, the entire group inevitably ends up in the kitchen. For the same unarticulated reasons, my daughter and her friends often end up underfoot here, even though the house has many other rooms.

My shrine is made up of Goddess statuary from all over the world, as well as figures of mothers with children from different cultures; a hammered tin shrine of the Virgin of Guadelupe, a gift from my friend Claudia, sits next to an African Ashanti wood statue of a nursing mother. Some of the images—the Goddess of Willendorf, the original of which may be 30,000 years old, and the Lespugue Goddess, created roughly 25,000 years ago—stand in plants, stuck into earth as they were intended to be thousands of years ago. In between, there are carved wooden animals, blue faience hippos from ancient Egypt, and small objects made by my only child, whose baby picture is in the very center. Every single object on the ledge has personal resonance; the animals are there because I have both a keen interest in animals and a real sense of connection to them. The shrine took shape gradually as a reflection of the growth of my own interest in ancient feminine spirituality. Because my role as a mother (and a cook) often requires that I give up the interests of the self (finishing work or writing), the shrine is a place of strength for me. It reminds me that the continuity of mothers and daughters itself is sacral in nature and that the ordinary, day-to-day acts of feeding my family and giving them my energies are meaningful. The images of women, mothers all, are a source of company and comfort. Though I often light candles, it is, for me, less a place of ritual than a still point for reflection and sustenance.

Creating Sacred Space

Bringing the sacred into the everyday, carving out sacred space in the domestic sphere, can be done in any number of ways and may serve more than one need. Eight thousand years ago, women and men placed small figurines of goddesses into their domestic grain bins to assure that there would never be a shortage of food; today, candles are lit and incense is burned on shelves in homes with a single figure of a Buddha, perhaps the goddess Kuan Yin, or the Virgin Mary to ask that life go on fully in any number of ways. Cindy, a photographer, has two altars in her West Coast home, each of which plays a different spiritual role in her life.

The first of her altars is in the main room of her house, the living room, and is built on the hearth of her fireplace. It is large and is the visual center of the room. Even though she was raised a Protestant, her own rituals are now Earth-focused, and the symbols on her altar draw on both the ancient iconography of the Goddess and Native American traditions, for she has traveled extensively in Europe and the

United States, photographing sacred sites. The altar's placement is dictated by a loose combination of the principles of *feng shui* (see "Deciding Placement, page 19) and the cardinal points used by the Native Americans; thus, it faces the front door, permitting the energy, or *chi*, to come in, as outlined in *feng shui*.

The basic altar consists of a mat woven by the Navajo that was given to Cindy after she photographed sacred rites on a reservation. Seated on it is a six-inch, pit-fired Goddess from Glastonbury in England, surrounded by candles and incense burners. An octagonal mirror, symbolic of water, is placed across from the altar to reflect its energy. Cindy has placed found, natural objects—stones, shells, and bits of wood—on the altar, their colors (black, white, and brown) deliberately arranged to reflect balance. The natural objects on the altar are replaced quarterly—at the equinoxes and solstices—when Cindy purifies the altar by building a fire in the fireplace and by washing all the elements.

To activate her altar, Cindy brings flowers and other found objects. Sometimes, as a way of visualizing a goal or need, she will bring a drawing or a photograph to the altar, or a thing of beauty she is particularly drawn to, as a way of focusing her own creative energy. She finds that smudge-burning or sprinkling water on the altar concentrates *its* energies as well as her own. Cindy's husband, friends, and relatives are invited to participate in altar rituals, as well as to use it alone as a resource of energy and strength.

The second altar in Cindy's home is far more personal and intimate, and for that reason it is placed on a dresser top in the bedroom. Unlike the living room altar, this is a place specifically for prayer. A simple shrine, it addresses what has become a pressing problem for Cindy (now in her forties) and many of her friends: aging, and often ailing, parents. The dresser is covered in a blue silk cloth, chosen for its color, symbolic of the waters and the skies. There are always flowers in a small vase here and some candles. Most important are the affirmations written on small pieces of paper that Cindy and her husband leave here as prayers for the strength and health of their loved ones.

Choosing the Room for Your Altar

Available space as well as convenience may be the primary factors that determine where you decide to put your altar or shrine; many people simply choose the room or area of their home they spend the most time in. How private—or how public—you wish your sacred space to be is another factor you may want to consider. Nancy Blair feels that an altar should be placed where the energy is needed; like many people who create altars, she tends to work intuitively rather than follow any system. Oralee Stiles, a spiritual director who designs altars, ceremonies, and rituals for other people, suggests that at least one altar in your home be visible from your bed, a safe haven of thought and quiet for many people, a place where you both begin and end your day.

No room should be considered inappropriate for sacred space. Many people, myself included, have sacred space in their kitchens, a gesture that hearkens back through the millennia when the hearth was the center of the home and the spiritual universe, where the gods and goddesses were honored and the fires were kept burning. The threshold of the home is also traditionally a place where sacred objects are kept to demarcate between the outside world and the world within, the profane and the sacrality of the hearth. For that reason, there is a small grouping of statuary and stones near Ed's front door, both an invitation to and an indication of the sacred space within.

Remember that the scale of your sacred space is entirely up to you; it need not be large or visually intrusive to affect your life and well-being.

Deciding Placement

Where to place your shrine or altar and how to orient it is, of course, a matter of personal choice. But your choice may be influenced by various philosophies that address the extent to which the sacred can be brought to infuse and invigorate both the home and the home altar.

Perhaps the simplest way of orienting your altar is by using the four directions or cardinal points. Many people like this approach simply because it links interior sacred space to the natural world outside, as well as to the sun, the moon, and the stars. Different cultures associate different qualities with the four directions; feel free to draw on your own associations as well.

In the most general terms, the North is often considered the realm of thought, of coolness and clarity, while the South is the area of passion, growth, heat, and light. The East is the place of the rising sun, and therefore the area of possibility and promise, often associated with enlightenment, wisdom, and the contemplative life. In contrast, the West is the area of the setting sun, of quiet and resolution, of activity and materialism, and of old age. Sufi journeys start in the west, a necessary step before turning east to gain spiritual knowledge. In some cultures, the axis from north to south represents potential, and the east to west is the axis of manifestation.

Feng shui, a mystical art of placement thousands of years old and long a part of living in China, has attracted many students in recent years. *Feng shui* means "wind" and "water" and is considered by the Chinese to be the force responsible for determining outcomes, health, prosperity, and good luck. *Feng shui* recognizes that all things have energy, or *chi.* In this philosophy, structures, buildings, and interior space are not inanimate but have energy all their own, which in turn affects the well-being and energy of their inhabitants.

Chi is energy, or the life force, in its broadest sense; it animates *all* things. Without *chi,* flowers will not bloom, rivers cannot flow, humanity cannot become. *Chi* determines the height of mountains, the quality of the flower, and all human potential and fulfillment. In Chinese philosophy, *chi,* or the life force, is made up of five elements: fire, metal, water, wood, and earth. In *feng shui,* these five elements are in turn combined with the cardinal points to bring energy, prayer, and good fortune to their optimum levels. The art of *feng shui* has been brought to bear on altar and shrine building in much the same way as the Native American medicine wheel.

Like the medicine wheel, which varies in its specifics from tribe to tribe and from one native culture to another, *feng shui* varies from one region of China to another. Underlying the art of placement, though, is a constant: the Chinese philosophy of yin and yang, symbolized by an S-curve of black and white with each side punctuated by a circle of the opposite color. The yin and yang symbol expresses the composition of life as a dynamic of opposing yet interconnected forces: light and dark, male and female, summer and winter, moon and sun, sinking and rising, cyclical and linear, cold and hot, inward and outward, dry and moist, and so on. The circle within each half symbolizes the opposite that each part of the dualism contains within its heart.

The balance of the forces of yin and yang is necessary for the individual to maintain harmony and health not only within the self but in domestic space as well. Because everything in a room contains either yin or yang or a combination of both, balance is critical. A room painted a dark color with little natural light has an overabundance of yin and, as those who have ever experienced living in a small, dark place can confirm, will make you tired and even ill; on the opposite spectrum, a very bright room with too much heat will sap energy by being overpowering.

For Frank, who has AIDS, balance as symbolized by the yin and yang has literal physiological meaning as well as spiritual resonance, and *feng shui* has influenced the placement of his altar in his New York studio apartment. His altar is a simple shelf, near where he works, placed in a direct route from the doorway so that *chi* can enter in; on it are a candle, a seashell that carries personal meaning, a drawing of a divinity, and a photograph. Frank will often add flowers or a crystal to enrich the energy of the altar. From time to time, he has moved the altar to keep the energies in his studio in balance and to maximize its power as a place of meditation that honors something larger than the self.

Precisely because *feng shui* has many variants, there are different ways of benefiting from and using its teachings; please consult the Resources section for sources of detailed information about *feng shui*. Following are some of the different approaches that offer possibilities for maximizing the energy potential of your domestic spiritual space:

Shapes. Linear shapes—rectangles and squares—are yang in nature and thus spin off energy. They should be balanced by circular, or yin shapes—in the form of objects or furniture—to keep the space in balance.

Doors and windows. Where you enter your home is important to the energy of the whole house, as well as to your altar or shrine. The *chi,* or energy, should be able to flow into the house as a whole; if the entrance is cramped, use mirrors to reflect *chi* back through the house. Mirrors should also be used to refract all the available light from windows to increase energy. *Feng shui* also holds that objects that protrude into space—columns, pillars, or exposed beams, for example—obstruct energy and that their negative effect on the flow of *chi* should be countered by wrapping the obstruction in cloth or by using mirrors to reflect *chi* onto another path and so through the dwelling.

Living things. Plants and potted flowers increase the energy in space, as do aquariums and terraria.

Moving objects. Wind chimes, mobiles, and running water, as in a small fountain, increase energy in domestic space.

Directions. The placement of elements within your home, including your shrine or altar, has significance in *feng shui*. In a grid called the *bagua,* drawn from the *I Ching,* the four cardinal points—South, West, North, and East—are related to four of the five elements, with the fifth element, earth, at the center. According to *feng shui,* both the cardinal points and the elements can be used to maximize the energy, or *chi,* of an altar or shrine. The *bagua* is often presented not simply in terms of the directions, but in terms of the parts of life the directions govern. For simplicity's sake, I use both below; please consult the Resources section for sources of detailed information on implementing the *bagua.*

South, or Illumination. The most important and auspicious of the cardinal points, South is associated with professional success, fortune, and fame, as well as with the warmth of the sun and the fecundity of summer. The element of fire is associated with the South, as is heat; the color red, the color of celebration in Chinese philosophy, is South as well. Facing your shrine or altar south and incorporating red objects is thought to increase the energy for attaining professional success. Birds are associated with this area.

West, or Creativity. The direction connected to autumn, West has a sphere of influence that includes joy and children. Metals are associated with the West, as is the color white, which in other contexts is considered an unlucky color. The white tiger is the animal associated with the West.

North, or the Journey or Career Path. The opposite of South, North is a complicated direction. On the one hand, North governs many of life's negatives, such as death and calamity; on the other, its element is water, and its animal is the tortoise, symbol of long life. Because the flow of water represents money in *feng shui*, the North is associated with business and career.

East, or Elders. Harmony and involvement in family life is the sphere of the East, as are health and well-being. Spring is its season, and the color green, symbolic of growth, is part of the East's domain. Wood is its element; the dragon, symbol of power and growth, is its animal. Use something green on your altar or shrine (a green candle, for example, or a plant) to maximize the possibilities of renewal in your personal and family life.

Midpoints between the cardinal points are also significant, depending on your spiritual needs; altars that address specific issues in your life might be oriented according to these areas.

Southwest, or Relationships. Southwest governs all partnerships, including marriage, motherhood, and sibling relationships. Its color is yellow.

Southeast, or Fortunate Blessings. Southeast is the domain of wealth and fortune; its color is purple.

Northeast, or Contemplation. Northeast is the area of intelligence, knowledge, and learning. Its color is blue.

Northwest, or Helpful Friends. Northwest is the domain of fatherhood and guardian spirits. This is considered an auspicious direction for those in need of spiritual support and sustenance and is, according to Denise Linn, a good place to put an altar. It is also the direction pertaining to travel.

The ideas of balance and harmony are essential to *feng shui*. The five elements—water, wood, fire, earth, and metal—also need to be connected in a creative rather than a destructive cycle of energy.

Other spiritual systems can be used to increase the energy of domestic sacred space. Sarah Teofanov, an artist whose spirituality is centered in women's mythology and the Earth, considers her entire house and the ground on which it stands to be sacred space. Inspired by Native American beliefs, she has altars in every room of her Victorian house as well as in her yard. The main living room and dining room altars are on mantelpieces and are decorated with stones, found bird feathers, candles, and statues of women and goddesses. Traditional altar houses made by a fellow artist who lived in Seattle are in her hallway and living room, surrounded by offerings of stones and seashells. In her kitchen window is a hanging shrine of found objects and figures of goddesses; her studio has an altar as well. Each of her altars has an orientation with both the cardinal points and the elements: she associates the East with Air, the South with Fire, the West with Water, and the North with the Earth.

The cardinal points—North, South, East, and West—along with the sky (up) and the earth (down) are also linked to the Native American medicine wheel, another possible guide to placing and orienting your shrine or altar. Like *feng shui,* the medicine wheel has many variants and is therefore best used as a source of guidance and inspiration rather than a set of rules to follow. The medicine wheel began as part of outdoor rites; in its earliest form it was probably a simple circle of stones set into the earth representing the Wheel of Life that sits below Father Sky and on Mother Earth. Most important is to understand that, as in all Native American thought, the medicine wheel assumes that there is no distinction between the sacred and the profane: the universe is animated by supernatural principles that are interconnected and in harmony. The role of ritual is to bring the individual or tribe into harmony with the Wheel of Life, which is larger and contains within it all living beings. Different tribes associate different totemic animals and birds with the directions, as well as colors, gemstones, vegetation, and gods and tutelary spirits. According to Gladys Reichard, among the Navajo, the east was associated with white, the white shell, the pigeon, and white corn; the south with blue, turquoise, the blue bird, and blue corn; the west with yellow, abalone, the yellow warbler, and yellow corn; the north with black, jet, the blackbird, and variegated corn. In the sections that follow, I have used the animals and stones and associations from Brooke Medicine Eagle's *Buffalo Woman Comes Singing;* for more on totemic animals to empower you and your sacred space, please see page 117, and for more on gemstones and minerals, page 107.

In the tradition of the medicine wheel, the four directions can be understood as follows:

East. The direction of the dawn, East is also the place of enlightenment and new knowledge; an altar facing east will draw on burgeoning power. It is also the direction of spring and growth, birth and childhood. Its color is yellow, its stone amber, and its animal the golden eagle.

West. The place of the setting sun and the moment between day and night, West is the direction of contemplation. Associated with the autumn, which lies between summer and winter, West is the place both of harvest and of letting go. It is the direction we face when we are ready to begin the journey into self-discovery. Its colors are the deepest of browns and black, and its stone is obsidian. Its totemic animal is sometimes the bear or the raven.

South. The place of the sun high in the sky and of the lush growth of summer, South indicates activity and productivity. It is an empowering direction to maximize the energy you need to follow an already chosen path. Its colors are red and sometimes green. Its animal is the coyote.

North. The crystal clarity of the winter sky is the North's. It is the direction of internalization and quiet, the place where we burrow deep beneath the frozen ground of the self and come back up with true self-knowledge and wisdom. It is the balancing direction to the hot energy and activity of the South. Its stone is the crystal and animal the white owl. Face your altar north to begin a journey of self-discovery and give it time to take shape.

The medicine wheel can be used to orient your shrine or altar or can be used as an element on the altar itself, for the circle is a powerful symbol of unity, harmony, and life. You can draw the medicine wheel, or you can sew one onto cloth and use it as part of your rituals. For outdoor rituals honoring the earth and the cosmos, the medicine wheel can be made out of stone. For more, see page 179.

Thresholds and hallways—the traditional entrances into the home—are wonderful places to create sacred space and to articulate the spirits of the home and its inhabitants. This wondrous altar is one of the first things you see as you enter Sarah Teofanov's home. Set on an exquisitely carved table, a traditional Raku spirit house created by Lalada Dalgish, a Brazilian artist living in Seattle, is surrounded by beautiful stones, draped with a glorious woven fabric, and made to sparkle with beads. In front of the spirit house are three small spiders, weavers of the web of life. To the left is a ceramic figure of a Mother Goddess created by Sarah herself. The lower part of the table is filled with specially chosen rocks and pebbles.

Creating Altars for Special Needs

Altars can be also be built to celebrate, commemorate, or mark turning points in one's life, to help heal grief or pain, or simply to focus energy on a specific part of life that needs attention. Leslie, a freelance writer who, in recent years, has written extensively on gardening and nature, found not only that new assignments were coming more slowly for her but also that she herself had slowed up and needed to concentrate her energies more on obtaining new work. To lessen her increasing sense of distraction, she set about cleaning her work space, filing papers and putting her books in order, and, finally, giving the room a fresh coat of paint to signify new beginnings. She also decided to build an altar on the top of her computer hutch that would serve as a point of inspiration and focus for her writing.

She began by grouping some meaningful and special books at the back of the shelf, largely books of poetry. Because the women in her life have inspired her, she placed photographs of her late grandmother and her mother, who died when Leslie was a teenager, in prominent places on the altar. The photo of her mother pictures her with Leslie and her younger sister. The last photograph, a tiny one enclosed in a silver frame decorated by a hummingbird, is of Leslie's own daughter and is perched up on a miniature typewriter Leslie found at a tag sale and bought simply because she loved it. The rest of the altar is filled with objects that have personal resonance for Leslie: an old milk can filled with dry hydrangeas, a postcard of a Japanese rendering of a delicate dragonfly, and a bird's nest that Leslie watched a wren build in a flowerpot on her porch some years ago and that she saved. Inside the bird's nest nestle two tiny scrolls, each tied with a gold cord, that were originally in a blessing pot Leslie's sister gave her. Each of the blessings, one written by Leslie and the other by her sister, concerns writing. Leaning against the picture of her grandmother is a sand dollar Leslie found on the beach on Cumberland Island where she was completing a writing assignment after a devastating period in her life. The fragile sand dollar is a symbol both of the ocean's waters she loves and of hopefulness. Above the altar, hung from the lamp that illuminates the work space, is a papier-mâché image of a young, nude boy riding a dolphin. Leslie bought this image last summer simply because "it spoke to me." She is not entirely sure why she has included it in her altar space, but, as she says, "It feels right."

Building an altar can also help you work through emotional pain. Oralee Stiles tells a story in the workshops and talks she gives that has helped many other people understand how to benefit from sacred space. Oralee was crushed when a close woman friend confessed that she had betrayed her. Rather than putting it out of her mind or simply letting her emotions wash over her, Oralee wanted to acknowledge the tremendous pain of the betrayal. Together, she and her friend built an altar out of an old cardboard box filled with objects symbolic of the destructive power of betrayal. Oralee broke a dish her friend had given her and placed its shards on the altar, along with a photograph, now torn in two, of the two women together. A lily—with one blossom in glorious full bloom, one in bud, and two blossoms browned and withered—was placed on the altar to symbolize all the stages of life. The two women spent time with the altar, and Oralee felt herself moving through her feelings, the pain no longer raw yet, at the same time, fully acknowledged. It was at that point that she could let go of what happened between them and go forward; it had, in Oralee's words, "become a story."

Altars can also commemorate and help the process of mourning and grieving, whether the grief involves the loss of a relationship or the death of a friend. Ann Evans created an altar when her friend Eszike died, to work through both her grief and, in Ann's words, her "need to remember her in my life." The altar was built out of things that had belonged to Eszike and that permitted Ann to hold on to her—her extraordinary and sometimes outrageous jewelry, the incredible fabrics she created, the gardenias she always had in the house. The altar both comforted Ann in her loss and, at the time, permitted her to recognize the many roles her friend had played in her life. Ann has decided to keep the altar up for one year.

The first thing artist and ritualist Sarah Teofanov did when she learned of the death of her friend Scott Fisher on a mountain-climbing expedition on Mount Everest was to build an altar. As she explained it to me, the altar performed a threefold service. First, the altar, deliberately built in a public area of her home, alerted the community to the fact that something had happened, much the way veiled mirrors or ribbons or armbands do. Second, the altar was a physical place to recognize her relationship to Scott and to his surviving family. Last, it was a vehicle for coming to terms with a terrible loss and tragedy. The altar was built over the course of a month, and the natural elements on it— the flowers and petals—ebbed and flowed and transformed themselves, just as the altar itself transformed Sarah's feelings and understanding.

....

Workplace Altars

Our society is comfortable distinguishing between "professional" and "personal" lives just as if most people have two totally separate selves, one eternally clad in a suit for the office and the other in sweats or jeans for time at home. In fact, though we may choose, in the workplace, to keep the details of our personal lives private, there is only one self, dividing its time between work and home, often struggling to keep the pressures or stresses from one area of endeavor from impinging on the other. For many people who work in high-rise offices and are literally cut off from fresh air and trees and anything natural for hours at a time, sometimes even losing sight of the sky and the weather in windowless cubicles, creating sacred space in the workplace is as important and valuable—perhaps even more so—as it is in the home. Incorporating a small-scale altar into the workplace is a reminder, too, that our spiritual needs should be tended to no matter where we are physically.

The workplace altar does not have to be large to be effective. You should decide beforehand whether you will want to answer questions about your altar posed by colleagues or if you want it to blend smoothly into the workplace surroundings. Begin by looking carefully at the space in which you work and how you use the space. Where do you usually sit, and what direction do you face? What do you usually look at? Is the space conducive to productivity, or is it dingy and depressing? Try to treat the space as if it matters to you (you spend enough time there, after all); straighten and neaten, and file or throw out papers or documents you no longer need. Then, choose a place for your sacred space based on your own needs. For example, if you spend long hours on the telephone or in front of a computer screen, pick a spot where you can literally turn away from your work for a moment to rest your eyes and your spirit during the workday. If you work in an office with a window, using the windowsill for your altar has the added benefit of opening up your vistas in a literal way. You can choose objects for your altar that remind you of the things within you and in your life that nurture your spirit. One woman I know uses a photograph of a flowering cherry tree and a pond that she took on one of her trips through the countryside. These are perched on the windowsill behind her desk, along with a small bowl filled with pebbles and shells. The photograph and bowl, framed by the sky, act like a spiritual tonic and help calm her when she's feeling overwhelmed by work or simply tired. You can affirm your spirit, too, by using words or a saying on your altar, something that reminds you of what really matters.

You can also build a workplace altar to energize the space you spend over forty hours a week in. Try working with some of the principles of *feng shui,* incorporating a plant or a small aquarium with a single goldfish in it to raise the energy level in your office. The simple addition of a few fresh flowers, particularly scented ones, will automatically raise your spirits and energy, and provide a focal point for a moment of quiet during the bustle of the day. Natural objects—a shell or a small crystal—can act as visual reminders of the natural world outside and the ebb and flow of all things, including the occasional work-related crisis. Sacred imagery—a statue of Athena, for example, for invention or an image of a wolf for leadership—can be used to help you maximize your strengths; equally, other images—a Kuan Yin for compassion or a snake for energy and transformation—can keep you focused on qualities you strive to incorporate into your working day. If your job requires that you work closely with other people, try building an altar that supports partnership, choosing pairs of objects or a symbol—such as a knot—signifying interdependence, along with images of fruition. If your working space, like so many, has been designed with sterile colors, try working with color on your altar to change the energy level; choose brightly colored objects for high energy, softly colored ones for a calming effect.

Any object with personal resonance—the memento of a trip or an emotionally important occasion, a photograph of a loved one—is a powerful visual reminder that our lives are filled with many gifts. Try choosing things that remind you of the fullness of life. Objects that can be handled—a small string of beads, the round smoothness of a rock or mineral, the soft fragility of a feather—are a way of bolstering yourself with the power of touch. Scent also has the ability to evoke feeling and thoughts; put a pinecone on your altar or scatter a few dried rose petals or fill a small bowl with potpourri.

Carving out a bit of sacred space in the office—no matter how small or unobtrusive—is an important reminder that the various dualisms or bifurcations our society encourages us to believe in—the separation of the sacred and the profane, the intellect and the spirit, the mind and the body, the professional and the personal—are really not helpful if we intend to live productive, fulfilled, and spiritually rewarding lives. By creating sacred space where we work, we signify our presence there and our intention to use the time we spend at work as fruitfully as possible.

Portable Altars

Creating sacred space need not be limited to the home or the office but can be accomplished in the most temporary of surroundings. The diminutive scale of some of the oldest of humanity's sacred objects reminds us that the idea of portable sacred space is perhaps as old as worship itself. The 30,000-year-old Willendorf Goddess, for example, stands only slightly over four inches high, fitting comfortably in the hand; her scale tells us she was a personal spiritual artifact rather than one connected to communal rites. The sizes of the other Goddess figurines that have survived the passage of the millennia—the 20,000-year-old, five-and-a-half-inch Lespugue Goddess carved out of mammoth ivory and the stylized figurine carved out of coal, some 16,000 years ago, at a scant inch and three quarters, for example— confirm the observation. Many of these images, too, have legs that end in points, suggesting that they may have been stuck into the ground or perhaps the wood of a tree as a part of personal ritual or prayer. For millennia, the power of the image itself to confirm and acknowledge the presence of the divine simply underscored the sacrality of all space—from the cave and the mountain to the threshold of the home to the bread oven and, finally, to the grave.

Throughout human history, sacred space has continued to be created in permanent settings with formal arrangements of large-scale ritual objects and furniture, such as altars and benches, as well as impermanent ones with smaller-scale, portable versions of sacred objects. Just as today, 20,000 years ago pendants or objects worn on or close to the body were thought to confer protection or act as an acknowledgment of the power of the divine. An exquisite mammoth ivory bead, perforated so as to be worn and carved in the shape of a neck and two breasts, striated to indicate moisture, has survived from Dolni Vestonice in what was formerly Czechoslovakia; even though it is only one inch long, it doubtless conferred upon its wearer the life-nourishing protection of the Great Mother. Thousands of years later, a tiny, miniaturized version of the Minoan double ax, rendered in gold with its handle reduced to the width of a pin, brought the person who carried it in a pocket or pouch similar benefits.

All over the world, amulets act, in effect, as portable sacred space, signifying the individual's intent to honor the deity and to invoke his or her protection against all manner of evil and ill fortune. In ancient Egypt, the amulet was omnipresent through life and death, worn on the bodies of the living and the mummified remains of the dead alike. The *ded,* or pillar representing the backbone of Osiris—hence his re-birth—was buried with the dead to ensure safe entrance into the netherworld; another pillar-shaped amulet, this one made of carnelian, was dedicated to Isis with the words "O blood of Isis, O splendor of Isis, O magic power of Isis, O amulet for protection." The wearing of the amulet guaranteed Isis's favor and protection and the individual's rebirth. Key-shaped amulets were important to both the Greeks and the Romans, invoking, respectively, Apollo and Diana, and Janus and Jana. The key signified both remembrance of the past and the fore-sight of the future; it was also a symbol of the sacred threshold. The Roman Janus, the two-faced god who looked both directly into the past and into the future, held the key to the door through which prayers had access to the gods; Jana was a protector of new life as well as light. Wearing an amulet key, particularly one made of silver, the metal of the moon, on a ring or necklace or carrying one brought the presence of the deities into personal, physical space.

A portable or traveling altar can be simplicity itself: a printed image or a small-scale statue, a few stones or a crystal, a small piece of cloth. Once again, the ancient human impulse to create meaningful space, to make ourselves spiritually and emotionally at home wherever we are, sometimes reveals itself long before the individual is conscious of the true meaning of his or her actions. Long before she ever heard of altars or altar building, almost twenty years ago, Caroline carried a lace handkerchief with a small statue of the Willendorf Goddess tucked inside it wherever she went. An unfamiliar room would become familiar with the handkerchief and image on a table or dresser. Similarly, for my first stay in a hospital, when my daughter was born, I packed and set up what I only now recognize to be an altar next to my hospital bed. In addition to pictures of my husband, dog, and cat, I brought along a seashell, a reproduction of an ancient Egyptian hippopotamus, and a carved effigy of a sheep.

The most dreary of hotel rooms, far away from home, can be changed by the creation of sacred space. If you are traveling on business, bring just a few small things that will help support and nurture your spirit; the addition of a few flowers placed in a glass or a small, scented votive candle will raise your energy after a long day of talk and work. Creating sacred space helps center and ground us, reminding us of *who* we are, no matter where we are.

Choosing Materials

What you use to create your altar will probably have a lot to do with the materials you have on hand and, of course, available surfaces and limitations of space. You may want to consider some of these symbolic histories as you begin to choose the primary elements for your sacred space. Keep in mind, though, that you need not be literal-minded; you don't have to build your entire altar out of stone to evoke its power. The presence of a small stone or rock on your altar, for instance, can be used as the beginning of a meditation on permanence, the eternal, or the Earth Mother, or to simply communicate a deity's presence.

You may also wish to take a look at the "Altar Ware" section on page 57.

Clay. In Native American and other cultures, clay and pottery are sacred in nature, for they are perceived as being endowed with life. The many metaphors of the potter and clay—including the one recounted in Genesis—that animate origin myths all over the world make it clear that clay, creation, and reproduction are often synonymous, and usually associated with the feminine. In the Assyrian myth that predates Genesis, the goddess Manu, or Mami, created humanity out of clay. Among the Pueblo Indians, figurines of raw and baked clay were buried in rites of increase.

Clay and pottery are often strongly associated with the feminine. Clay is an earth material, transformed by fire, and thus has great spiritual resonance.

Mirror. Mirrors or their equivalents—highly polished pieces of stone—have long been understood as magical in power, associated with the moon and water, and capable of reflecting truth and the soul within. The Aztecs used obsidian mirrors for divination; the name of their all-powerful god of the four directions, Tezcatlipoca, means "smoking mirror." In other cultures, too, the mirror is connected to the revelation of truth and the soul, both literally and metaphorically. The mirror of the Shinto goddess Amaterasu is one of the holy treasures kept in the Shrine of Ise in Japan. Amaterasu, the goddess of the sun, and her brother, the storm god Susanowo, were created at the same time. His rough behavior forced Amaterasu to withdraw into a cave, thus depriving the world of light. Only by music, dance, and a mirror—which reflected light back into the world—was her brightness restored.

On contemporary altars, many people incorporate mirrors to increase the energy of the altar, following the principles of *feng shui,* or as a symbol of reflection. Using a mirror in your sacred space will also make it seem larger; it is also possible to position a mirror to reflect certain elements—a hanging plant, the natural light—that you would like to be part of your sacred space.

Paper. Even though it is a perishable material and thus testifies to the fragility of life, paper is inextricably linked to the power of the word to transform and to bring the sacral into our presence. In the Shinto religion, folded pieces of paper form part of ritual; in Tibetan Buddhism, prayers written on paper are ritually burned so that the prayers, borne on whorls of smoke, reach the ears of the deities. Our word *paper* comes from the Egyptian papyrus, which, rolled and tied, signified knowledge.

Stone. Rocks and stones have, for millennia, symbolized divine power, as well as permanence, wholeness, and cohesion. The seemingly impervious nature of stone against the elements made it part of the eternal as well as a force of protection for both the living and the dead. In many cultures, rocks or stones were a sign of the deity's presence, whether the Cretan Mother Goddess, worshiped both as a stone and a stalagmite, or the Roman Cybele, worshiped in the form of a black meteorite; "the House of God," or "Bethel," in the Old Testament; or the pairs of stones, male and female, worshiped by the ancient Hawaiians as ancestors. The essentially sacral nature of stone, articulated in many cultures, is firmly addressed in the Book of Exodus, which forbids altering stone in any way: "And if thou wilt make me an altar of stone, thou shalt not build it of hewn stone: for if thou lift up thy tool upon it, thou has polluted it" (Exodus 20:25).

As Marija Gimbutas has pointed out, for millennia, many cultures also perceived rocks and stones as the children of the Earth Mother, endowed with many of her life-giving and regenerative powers; dolmens and stones were part of fertility rites for thousands of years. In ancient Rome, large stones with flat surfaces, dedicated to the fertility goddess Ops Consui, were buried in the ground and covered with straw to be uncovered once a year during the harvest festival. As late as the nineteenth century, childless women in France would journey to the great standing stones, or menhirs, of Brittany to supplicate for fertility.

For more on stones, see "Sacred Stories," page 171.

Wood. Like the tree from which it comes (see page 147), wood is associated in many cultures with the sacred, for the tree was often the dwelling place of the god or goddess. Wood is also, in many cultures, the primordial matter; thus, in China, wood is one of the five elements. It corresponds to the east and to spring, to nature and manifestation. In the Celtic tradition, wood signified learning in all of its aspects, unless it was used in a funerary context; the Irish alphabet, therefore, was carved only in wood. In all the Celtic languages, the words for "learning" and "wood" share the same root.

Many people build their altars out of wood or on wood simply because it is of nature, its presence testimony to the greater cycle of life.

Cloth: Weaving and Sacrality

Many people use a cloth or fabric as the basis for their altar, an action that ties into a long sacral history. Both the act of weaving and the woven fabric (symbolically, the web) are ancient symbols of harmony and life, associated in many cultures with the moon and the feminine as well as goddesses; similarly, spinning and the thread itself also have symbolic and mythological resonance, mirrored in the three Greek Fates, or the Moirae, who spin, measure, and cut the thread of every person's life, and the Scandinavian Norns who do much the same thing.

As Elizabeth Wayland Barber has pointed out in her *Women's Work: The First 20,000 Years,* woven garments have been used both symbolically and ritually since Neolithic times. The string "skirts" that appear on many carved Goddess figurines, such as the Lespugue, may have symbolized fertility, while special pieces of cloth and clothing—the large "sacred knot" worn at the back of the neck by Minoan priestesses, for example—denoted participation in ritual activity. The ancient Egyptians, celebrated weavers of the finest of linens, adorned the figures of their gods and goddesses with fresh robes as part of their offerings, following the example of the goddess Isis, who wove garments for her husband, Osiris. In ancient Greece, the long months devoted to designing and weaving the sacred robe, or *peplos,* for the gold and ivory statue of Athena at the Parthenon, for the goddess's annual festival, was a way of focusing attention on devotion to the deity; the robe was carried with great ceremony by a huge procession of all Athenians, led by the young girls who had woven it. Cloth symbolized the sacred "web of life" associated with the feminine, "woven" from her body. It is in this context that we can understand the offerings given to the Greek goddess Artemis, patroness of childbirth: spindle whorls and loom weights. So strong were associations of weaving with the feminine that even the apocryphal legends surrounding the Virgin Mary depict her as weaving the purple veil or cloth for the temple as a young girl. In these legends, as she weaves, an angel comes to her and announces that she will bear a miraculous child.

Since ancient times, hanging or draped cloth, woven with symbolic patterns and, after the fourth millennium, dyed various colors, designated sacred and ritual space. The Book of Exodus details the rich hangings and fabrics left at the tabernacle as offerings: "And all the women that were wise hearted did spin with their hands, and brought that which they had spun, both of blue, and of purple, and of scarlet, and of fine linen" (Exodus 35:25).

Elsewhere in the world, weaving and fabric are also sacred. The Mayan moon goddess Ixchel is a weaver who taught humanity the art; among the Navajo, the same role is played by Spider Woman, who was often gifted with woven offerings. In Native American traditions, the Earth Mother is often portrayed as the first loom builder: she weaves a sacred blanket for the earth from which all the flora and the fauna emerge into being.

In many traditions, including Buddhism, beautifully brocaded or embroidered cloths adorn altars and sometimes are part of offerings. Julie Middleton, who loves fabrics and textiles, always begins her altar with a piece of fabric, which represents what she wants "the altar to do or be." One woman I know always puts a blue cloth on her altar, symbolic of water and sky, the depths of the ocean and the heights of heavens; she feels it clarifies her altar and permits her to focus on the work at hand. On the gratitude altar pictured on page 137, I used a piece of an antique obi, the traditional Japanese sash, because it was woven in earth colors—soft celadon green, browns, rusts, and blacks—and depicted cranes, symbols of long life and good luck, flying over pine trees.

You can also use the cloth on your altar as a symbol of interconnection, of life and the threads that bring us all together.

Perhaps most expressive of that thought is the Tewe prayer that sums up the power and beauty of woven things:

> O Our Mother the Earth, O Our Father the Sky
> Your children are we and with tired backs
> We bring you the gifts you love.
> Then weave for us a garment of brightness
> May the warp be the white light of morning
> May the weft be the red light of evening
> May the fringes be the falling rain
> May the border be the standing rainbow.
> Thus weave for us a garment of brightness
> That we may walk fittingly where grass is green
> O Our Mother the Earth, O Our Father the Sky.

....

Color and Its Meanings

As it always has, color plays an important role in ritual and ceremony the world over, for humanity has always understood color as containing potent magic that can affect the sensitivity and receptivity of the spirit within. What humanity has always intuited, science has proved: certain colors—reds, for example—have the ability to agitate and distract, whereas others—blues, for instance—calm us and open us up for thought. The combination of colors in the spaces we inhabit and work in affect us as well, as they will in your sacred space.

Working with color for your altar and sacred space should mirror your intent and your own personal associations, because color is perhaps the most complicated area of symbolism, varying from culture to culture all over the globe. The example of white is a telling one. Whether perceived as the presence of all colors in the spectrum or the total absence of color, white has markedly different associations. Up through the Neolithic, according to Marija Gimbutas in *The Language of the Goddess*, white was the color of death and bones, and black, now associated with death, was the color of fertility. By the time of the Greeks, though, white was associated with purity and innocence, as well with the new moon, Athena, and summer (*Leucosis*, or "the Whitening"). White animals were sacrificed to the deities of the heavens and black ones to those of the netherworld. In contrast, in Asia, white is a distinctly inauspicious color, the color of mourning. On the opposite spectrum, in Navajo rite, white is a naturally sacred color associated with the sun and maleness; white garments are indicative of spiritual readiness to connect with the divine.

The association of color with ritual practice also varies widely from culture to culture. In ancient Egypt, the cycle of life was represented by the colors green, red, white, and black. During the course of the year, statues of Osiris were painted different colors to symbolize a stage of the cycle. Red symbolized the shedding of Osiris's blood to fructify the earth; white stood for the nurturing milk of the Milky Way, or the goddess Hapi; black was the color of gestation, and green the color of vegetation. Thus, as the grain sprouted underground, Osiris was pictured as black and then repainted green with the appearance of the first shoots. The stepped ziggurats of ancient Mesopotamia were, according to E. O. James, painted in ascending colors, culminating in the highest ritual place: white, purple, black, red, silver, and gold. In Tibet, paintings of the Buddha include a tricolored border of red, yellow, and blue—with the blue band at the outermost edge of the painting—to separate the painted sacred objects from the material world.

In some cultures, colors are specifically associated with the cardinal directions or the elements. Once again, the symbolism varies. Among many Native American tribes, yellow was north; blue, west; red, south; and white, east. In Tibet, white equals space; blue, air; yellow, earth; red, light; and green, water.

Color can become an important part of ritual in your sacred space. Ann Evans's November altar, built for a group ritual, was meant to challenge and celebrate the participant's sense of the season, a time without great clarity when, as Ann says, the "connection to the other world is very thin, and we perceive ourselves going into the depths." On the altar, she placed a gold cloth that was then covered by black netting, symbolic of the time of illusion. Underneath the netting, half hidden, were symbolic objects: a tiny cauldron for the harvest goddess; a seashell for water; a black egg for night; a broom for the time of the crone; a porcelain snake to symbolize energy and "the slithering in between." Candles placed at the four directions were lighted, and a mirror was placed behind the altar to reflect the beauty of the divine feminine within each of the participants in the ritual.

As the brief sketches of color symbolism that follow make clear, there is no "right" way to use color. You may draw on the associations offered by various traditions, or follow your own heart. Color can be represented by minerals or gemstones, cloths and fabrics, bowls and plates, flowers, or candles. Colors work differently in combination: you can balance something red on your altar—signifying energy, passion, blood, or fruition—with blue—the color of sky, water, and contemplation. Green, a color I associate with the vital force of life and nature, is represented by the ivy plants that sit amid the statuary on my kitchen altar.

Black. Once the color of fertility and of the depths of the Mother Earth, now black is primarily the color of night, death, and the underworld, as well as of primal matter without form. It was once the color of the great goddesses—of Diana, Kali, and Isis—and the powers they wielded. Black continued to suggest a quality of mystery as well, for the protection the darkness offers; thus, for the Navajo, though black could be the color of the sinister, it was also a protective color because it conferred invisibility.

Blue. The color of the sky, the heavens, and the waters, blue is a cool color, often associated with the intellect as well as the spirit. Blue has been the attribute of both the masculine and the feminine, for gods and goddesses alike wear blue clothing; even the blue mantle of the Virgin Mary belongs to this tradition. In many cultures, blue is a protective color, used in amulets. In Tibetan Buddhism, blue symbolizes both potentiality and emptiness at once. For the Navajo, blue symbolizes the fructifying power of the earth and is associated with the direction south.

Brown. The color of the earth, brown—as the withering, browned leaves on branches and on the ground remind us—is also the color of the cycle of life from beginnings to endings. For the Romans and later the Christians, brown was also the color of humility.

Gray. The midpoint between black and white, gray is the color of mediation, as well as of passages. Though gray also carries the negative associations of mist and ashes, it is important to remember that all human beings begin, as newborns, by perceiving the world around them in shades of gray, differentiating objects colored black and white by their high contrast.

Green. In ancient Egypt, the color green was associated with Osiris and thus signified both life *and* death. Though green is often used as the color of rebirth and vitality, as well as hopefulness, it was also the color sacred to Venus and thus emblematic of love. For that reason, for centuries brides wore green. Green is also associated with the life-giving powers of water.

Purple (violet). A sacral color, purple is associated with the priests and priestesses at Eleusis, for example, as well as elsewhere. Purple is associated with temperance and deliberate action and, as a blend of red and blue, of the balance of heaven and earth and passion and reason.

Red. The color of blood, symbolic of life, red is perhaps the most sacred of colors and an important part of religious and spiritual symbolism the world over. Red is energy, strength, and sometimes healing. Associated with love and passion, as well as combat, red is the color of fire and connected to the planet Mars. It is the color of the womb and thus often associated with the feminine; red is the sacred color of the Hindu goddess Lakshmi, goddess of agriculture, good luck, and prosperity.

White. In addition to the associations mentioned earlier, white is also the color of initiation, of light, and of knowledge; the white lotus is an emblem of Buddha's knowledge. The Druids wore white as a holy color. White is also the color of milk, the primal food.

Yellow. Firmly associated with both the sun and the riches of the earth (gold), yellow is often connected to the spring and is variously a symbol of enlightenment and the intellect. In the Native American tradition, it is a female color, associated with the power of reproduction and growth, for the sacred pollen is yellow. In Buddhism, yellow—the color of the robes of the Buddha and all his priests—signifies renunciation of the world.

Statuary

Many of the sacred spaces described and pictured in this book include statuary or representations of deities from many traditions. Images of deities—whether they are iconic (representational) or aniconic (without features)—have long been part of human worship everywhere, and, throwing cultural prejudices aside, it is important to remember that the iconic is not more "civilized" or "advanced" than the aniconic. In most highly developed societies, in fact, the aniconic and iconic exist side by side as expressions of the divine.

These images are a reflection of divine power and therefore, in the context of sacred space, act as revelation of the nature of the divine. They are also a symbolic reminder of the deity's presence and nature and thus can provide a starting point for prayer and meditation that the individual can then transcend. They are a visual shorthand for what we need to remember about the sacred, and they present us with a way of understanding divine nature in relation to ourselves and our spiritual goals, whether the grounded compassion of the Buddha or Kuan Yin, or the all-embracing love of the Virgin Mary.

Contemporary interest in spirituality has brought wide availability of sacred objects from many different cultures—from beautiful reproductions of Goddess figures from the Paleolithic and Neolithic to sculptures of Athena and Hera to Shivas, Ganeshas, and Buddhas at every price range and in many materials. Describing all the imagery you might wish to place upon your altar is, of course, beyond the scope of this book, but I hope this listing will serve as a guide to those objects mentioned throughout the book.

Please consult Resources, page 203, for more information about obtaining sacred objects for your altar.

Aphrodite. Closely allied to the sea—for she was born out of the foam of the waters—Aphrodite is the Greek goddess of love, marriage, and beauty. She is also the goddess of joy, attended by the three Graces (Euphrosyne, or Joyfulness; Aglaia, or Brilliance; and Thalia, or Bloom), and wherever Aphrodite is present, she kindles or rekindles love and passion and generates new life.

Artemis. Greek goddess of nature and the untamed wilderness, Mistress of the Animals, the virgin goddess Artemis also protected women in childbirth. Artemis too was a goddess of fertility, though only of animals, not vegetation. Untouched and unsullied, yet intricately connected to the cycle of life, she is the wilderness within each woman.

Athena. Her name, Athena, which means simply "a goddess" (*a thea*), betrays her roots, which reach back far into the Paleolithic and Neolithic, when, in Merlin Stone's words, "God was a woman," although the Athena of the Greeks is born full-grown from the head of Zeus. She is first and foremost a goddess of intelligence and invention; her gifts to humanity include the bridle and the chariot, the rudder and the ship, weaving, and the olive tree. Her spirit is martial.

Bast. The Egyptian goddess of life and fruition and the Lady of the East, Bast is usually represented with a cat's head (and bearing a sistrum, representing rejuvenation) or with the head of a lioness surmounted by a snake. In earliest times, Bast was worshiped as a cat, and, according to E. A. Wallis Budge, she was also a personification or manifestation of the heat of the sun. Equally, though, she was a lunar goddess, associated with childbearing and fruitfulness.

Brahma. The Hindu creator of the world, Brahma is often portrayed with four heads facing the four directions, symbolic of the four Vedas. He is first and foremost the lord of wisdom. His wife Saravasti is the goddess of music.

Buddha. His name literally means "The Enlightened," and images representing the Buddha, or Siddhartha Gautama, the founder of Buddhism, abound on altars and in sanctuaries the world over. Up until the first century B.C.E., the Buddha was usually represented only in aniconic form or by a symbol or a combination of symbols (the Footprint, the Wheel of Law, the Lotus, the Bodhi Tree, or the Stupa, for example); humanized representations developed within a system of meaningful iconography, including a halo, rays of light, or flames representing the supreme Buddha Light, or wisdom, the *urna,* a small crystal or white curl symbolizing wisdom, as well as hand *mudras,* which indicate the activity of the Buddha. The preaching or teaching Buddha is shown with the *Dharmachakra-mudra,* the hands raised to the breast and fingers imitating the turning of the Wheel of Law, with the forefinger and thumb forming a circle. After his enlightenment, the Buddha touched the earth, shown in the *Bhumisparsha-mudra,* the fingertips of the right hand pointing down over the right knee. In the posture of meditation, the Buddha's hands are shown in the *Dhyana-*

mudra, overlapping with the palms up. As the Compassionate One and granter of favors, Buddha is depicted in the *Vara-mudra*, the hand held down with the palm up. Protective, the Buddha is shown in the *Abhaya-mudra*, with the left hand raised.

Cybele. The Magna Mater, or "Great Mother," usually portrayed as driving a chariot driven by lions, Cybele was the goddess of the sacred mountain, Mount Ida, and of fertility and wildlife and guardian of the dead. Originally a goddess of Anatolia, her worship first spread to ancient Greece and then to Rome, where it reached its fullest flowering. In 204 B.C.E., when Rome appeared to be losing its twelve-year battle against the invader Hannibal, the oracle of Delphi was consulted concerning a prophecy in the Sibylline books that said an invader could be vanquished if the Mother of Ida was brought to Rome. The priestess confirmed the prophecy, and arrangements were made to bring the black meteorite that embodied the goddess to Rome. After many travails (the specially built boat of pines hewn from Mount Ida was stranded on a sandbar, for example, but was saved miraculously by a Roman matron who prayed for Cybele's intervention), the stone arrived in Rome and was installed in the Temple of Victory. A year later, the prophecy fuflfilled itself: Hannibal was driven back, and the harvests were lush and full.

Demeter. The goddess of the earth's fruition (her name probably means "mother"), Demeter was the goddess of the fertile earth and grain; her daughter, Kore, or Persephone, symbolized the new harvest. The story of Persephone's abduction by Hades, lord of the underworld, her mother's terrible grief, and her eventual return to her mother and the earth for one-third of the year—a symbolic rendering of the vegetative cycle from growth, through harvest, to the dying off of the plants, to rebirth in the spring—was the focus of the Greek Eleusinian Mysteries.

Gaia, or Ge. The oldest of all the Greek goddesses, the earth itself, Gaia, or Ge, was born of Chaos and then created Uranus, god of the heavens, with whom she then mated to produced Cronus and the Titans. The supercession of Gaia's primacy in worship is retold in the myth of Apollo at Delphi. Delphi, the oracular center of Greece, was sacred to Gaia, who uttered prophecies in a rocky cave while guarded by her son, the serpent Pytho. Apollo killed the snake and claimed the holy oracle as his own.

Ganesh, or Ganesha. The son of Shiva, Ganesh, a god with the head and trunk of an elephant with tusks (one or both broken) and a rotund body, is often shown seated on a mouse or a flower; he symbolizes the potential of life, is the god of wisdom and learning, and is honored as the "remover of obstacles."

Hathor. The Egyptian goddess of the cosmos, creator and Queen of the Heavens and Mistress of the Underworld, Hathor is often represented with a cow's head or with a solar disk set between two curved horns. Goddess of the female principle, she is a patroness of women and of marriage. As a lunar goddess, she is also a deity of death, who is portrayed as feeding the souls of the dead from her sacred sycamore tree.

Hecate. A triple goddess of great power, associated with fertility and all three realms (earth, sky, and the underworld), the Greek Hecate presided over the crossroads of life, both literally and metaphorically; travelers would leave offerings to her at places where three roads met. Because her influence was felt everywhere, she was also associated with Selene, the moon in the heavens; with Artemis, the earthly huntress; and with Persephone, the goddess of the underworld. Her three faces of maid, mother, and crone were echoed in the first quarter moon, the full moon, and the dark or new moon. Eventually, her association with the underworld triumphed, and, for centuries, she was mainly identified as Queen of the Witches, an association now being slowly corrected as more people learn about the ancient feminine traditions.

Hera. Among the ancient Greeks, Hera, the sister and consort of Zeus, while portrayed in mythology as jealous and quarrelsome, was worshiped as Earth Mother, and her virginity was symbolically renewed each year in ritual at Argos. In the context of marriage, she was also a goddess of childbirth.

Hestia. The goddess of hearth and therefore of the home, Hestia was mentioned first by the ancient Greeks in all prayers and sacrifice, even when honoring another deity. Her fires were kept ever-burning, and with the establishment of every Greek colony, a sacred flame would be lighted from Hestia's hearth.

Inanna. The Sumerian Queen of Heaven, both the morning and the evening star, Inanna is also a fertile earth and grain goddess, whose epiphanies were the tree, the sycamore, the palm, the olive, and the apple tree, among others. Inanna's wisdom was the fabric of society; she gave it laws and its ordering principles. As in the cognate stories of Ishtar and Isis, Inanna's sacred marriage to Dumuzi, or Tammuz, reenacted each year in ritual, was a celebration of the rebirth of all vegetation.

Isis. The worship of Isis, originally a mother goddess of Egypt, would have a 3,000-year reign and would eventually spread through the ancient worlds of both Greece and Rome. Finally, in the first centuries of the common era, her worship was superseded by that of the Virgin Mary, who was to inherit many of her attributes. Precisely because she held a position of spiritual importance over the course of three millennia, she was worshiped in many ways, in many guises, and in many epiphanies: as an earth and fertility goddess; as a cow, snake, or bird goddess; as the loving mother of Horus, the sun god; as a goddess of the underworld; as the wife of Osiris, whose regenerated body assured the crops each season. She is often represented with outstretched wings, sometimes over the dead, and with a throne or house on her head.

Kuan Yin. The Chinese goddess of mercy, or "she who always hears prayers," Kuan Yin was until the twelfth century represented as a man, one of the Buddha's followers. Kuan Yin since then is often represented with a child in her arms and holding either a willow twig or a lotus blossom; in her other hand she usually holds a vase filled with the nectar of immortality. Many legends are told about Kuan Yin, but perhaps the most moving is the one that inspired her depiction with multiple arms, traditionally said to be one thousand, with the same number of eyes. Kuan Yin is the daughter of a sovereign who violently opposes her wish to join a monastery, so vehemently, in fact, that he intends to kill her if she persists. Kuan Yin is rescued by the lord of hell, Yama, who takes her to his domain of suffering, which Kuan Yin then transforms into a paradise. Yama releases her, and she is reborn on an island, where she protects sailors at sea. Her father, though, falls gravely ill, and Kuan Yin returns to him, offering the flesh of her arms to cure him. He recovers and orders a sculptor to carve a statue in her honor with "completely formed arms and eyes," but the sculptor misunderstands him and carves instead a figure with a thousand arms.

Lakshmi. In Hinduism, the spouse of Vishnu and a Mother Goddess, Lakshmi is associated with the lotus and with creative energy. She is the goddess of agriculture, fertility, wealth, prosperity, and good luck.

Nut. Wife of the Earth god Seb and mother of Osiris and Isis, the Egyptian goddess Nut rules over the heavens and sky, giving birth to the sun each morning and taking him back within her body each night, only to give birth again the following day. Sometimes conflated with Hathor, whose horns and solar disk she is shown wearing, as a protector of the dead, she is also represented in human form with a vase of water on her head.

Saint Cecilia. The patron saint of musicians, Saint Cecilia, a Christian, was unhappily betrothed to a pagan. As the musicians at her wedding played, Cecilia sang to God in her heart and converted her husband Valerian to Christianity. She was subsequently martyred.

Saint Francis of Assisi. His love for all of creation—for the birds, beasts, flowers, sky, and earth—has made Saint Francis of Assisi among the best loved and most revered of the saints, even among the devoutly secular, partly because of his exquisite hymn to "Brother Sun." People of all different beliefs use statues of Saint Francis in their sacred garden space.

Shiva, or Siva. A Hindu god of many diverse qualities—he is known by over one thousand names—Shiva is Creator, Preserver, and Destroyer at once and sometimes represented as three-faced. He is distinguished by his third eye, symbolic of spiritual vision, and his four arms, emblems of his mastery over the four directions. A god of fertility as well, he is often shown mounted on a white bull. In aniconic form, Shiva is represented by the *lingam,* the phallus, set within the *yoni,* representing the union of the male and female elements in nature. Teacher of yoga and patron of the ascetic orders, Shiva is also portrayed as *Nataraja,* lord of the cosmic dance; he is usually shown in a circle of flames, signifying eternal energy. He is arrayed in symbolic opposites: one hand holds the hourglass drum, the sound of time that counteracts the eternal, but in the other, he holds the flame of the eternal; in his hair, he has both a skull and a new moon, symbols of death and new life.

This exquisite large-scale altar, set in a meditation corner next to a gong and covered in a vibrant turquoise cloth, was created by Oralee Stiles. It has a Kuan Yin at its focal point, a child in her arms, set against a Japanese screen; she is surrounded by vases full of tulips, other representations of the divine feminine, and burning candles. For Oralee, this goddess of compassion represents as well the juggling act that is a woman's life, for she is usually portrayed holding something in her hands. A second Kuan Yin, this one represented with "a thousand arms," is on the lower tier of the altar, along with figures of rabbits. Bunnies and the goddess Kuan Yin are connected for Oralee; for her, they form an epiphany about "loving oneself."

Tara. The embodiment of compassion and bestower of blessings in Tibetan Buddhism, Tara appears in twenty-one forms, both beneficent and wrathful, each distinguished by different colors and iconography. Among the most popular is the Green Tara, who fosters growth and is a protectress in everyday life; the White Tara promises long life, health, and prosperity.

Tsao-wang. The Chinese kitchen god Tsao-wang, along with his wife, is guardian of the hearth and witnesses all that goes on in the family during the year; at year's end, he will allot the next year's fortune.

Virgin Mary. Certainly the most important female figure in Christianity, the Virgin Mary as a giver of loving-kindness and protection is beloved to Catholics the world over; the legatee of many traditions pertaining to the divine feminine, she has found her way into other hearts as well.

Vishnu. His name means "the Pervader," that which permeates all existence and through which everything exists. Both strong and compassionate, the Hindu god Vishnu is represented with four symbols: the conch shell (for water and the sound of creation), the lotus (for the unfolding universe), the mace (the power of knowledge conquering time), and the discus wheel (his weapon against evil).

Altar Ware: Jars, Bowls, and Containers

The burgeoning interest in altars and sacred space has, in the past few years, made many ritual objects drawn from different cultures readily available through stores or mail order sources. Exquisite reproductions of ancient ritual objects, offering bowls and specialized ceremonial implements from Tibet and Nepal, smudge pots from Native American cultures, as well as all manner of incense burners and candelabra are part of today's marketplace. It is difficult not to be tempted. One of the great pleasures, though, of creating an altar is looking through your own possessions with a new eye and bringing objects to the altar that really matter to you and resonate with meaning.

Even the shapes and forms of objects you can put on your altar often have symbolic meaning, sometimes readily available and sometimes lost in the mists of history. A closed box on your altar can symbolize mystery or the unknown, or it can indicate a treasure still hidden from view; equally, a closed box can be a place to keep small strips of paper with your innermost thoughts and desires. Take a close look at the things you have chosen to place on your altar, at their forms, their functions, their colors and decorations.

You may wish to bring some of the following ancient associations to your own altar as you begin to create your sacred space. Symbolically, many of these containers have primarily feminine meanings, although there are variations among them.

Basket. For the ancient Egyptians, as a hieroglyph, the basket symbolized the wholeness in divinity, for Isis gathered the scattered limbs of Osiris in a basket. The weaving of baskets, like that of cloth, is associated with the feminine as well as with the activity of women; thus, ceremonies dedicated to Greek and Roman goddesses such as Isis and Artemis included sacral baskets. In other cultures, too, baskets have profound meaning; in Buddhism, the canon of scriptures is called the *Tripitaka,* literally "the three baskets." Baskets in the Native American tradition were part of ceremony; the number of baskets used and their design and decoration were prescribed by ritual.

Use a basket on your altar to symbolize harvest or the act of gathering, or the interwoven nature of wholeness.

Bowl. Essentially feminine in nature, the open bowl, according to Erich Neumann's *The Great Mother,* carries with it the ideas of both containment and nourishment; its openness "accents the motif of giving, donating." Not surprisingly, the bowl is associated with the breast.

In addition to being ideal for offerings of food and water, use a bowl to gather blessings—either symbolic or written down on paper.

Box. The most famous "box" in Western mythology—the one Pandora was said to have opened, thereby releasing all of the ills that plague humanity into the world and putting responsibility for that action into female hands—was not, until the misogynist Hesiod retold the story and Erasmus mistranslated it, a box at all. (Originally, Pandora—whose name means "all gifts"—was the goddess herself, holding the *pithos,* or jar of life.)

The closed box is a symbol of the unconscious or the unknown.

Candelabra or candlesticks. The lighted candle symbolizes spiritual illumination and the number of branches on a candelabrum usually has a mystical significance. For more information, see "Fire, Light, and Smoke," page 90.

Cauldron. Though the cauldron is often linked with black magic and witchcraft, in fact, it was a holy object with complicated associations in different cultures. Usually, it was associated with transformation and rebirth. In the Celtic tradition, there were three cauldrons of importance. The first was the cauldron of plenty, which functioned in the same way as the Greek cornucopia, the source of all fruits and nourishment. The second cauldron was that of rebirth. The third was the sacrificial cauldron in which the dying king was ritually boiled. Mircea Eliade has argued that it is not the cauldron (or, for that matter, the kettle or any other vessel) that has the power of magic, but rather the water inside it. In Greek myth and European folklore, the boiling cauldron confers immortality. According to Erich Neumann, the cauldron is a symbol of the Goddess's body as the agent of spiritual transformation.

Chalice or cup. As a vessel specifically designed for drinking, the cup itself is less important than either the liquid contained within it or the act of drinking itself. Perhaps underlying the complex symbolism pertaining to cups is the essentially sacral nature of liquids as well as the human need for liquids as sustenance, water being primary among them. Like the cornucopia (see page 64), the filled cup functions as a symbol of plenty, of the earth's gifts or a deity's beneficence; equally, it can symbolize human destiny, filled either with blessings or with bitterness. Drinking of the liquid the cup contains can be an act signifying the acquisition of knowledge or immortality, or it can be a gesture of thanksgiving or communion.

Jar. Like the bowl, the jar is associated with the feminine, specifically the life-giving liquids, water and milk. According to Erich Neumann, closed vessels such as the jar and the kettle (in contrast to the bowl or the goblet) carry "the creative aspect of the uterus and the potentiality of transformation." The great Egyptian goddess Isis is often portrayed with a jar around her neck, as is the god Osiris, while the river deities often carry jars from which waters flow. The jar is also womblike, and so, though Greek jars with two handles, or *amphorae,* were used to store olive oil and other foodstuffs, as symbols of rebirth, they were also burial places of the dead.

Pot. The pot too is connected symbolically to the womb in many places in the world; in India, it is a symbol of the goddess Kali. Because clay and pottery itself are closely connected to the feminine and Earth, the pot is also a symbol of Earth's body.

Urn. Urns with lids, as well as those mounted on pedestals or feet, have long been used for funerary purposes; symbolically, they are a dwelling or home for the soul from which the soul then emerges. The urn is also one of the Chinese Eight Treasures.

Vase. Vases with breasts and nipples, from the sixth millennium, decorated with meanders and most probably used for the ritual collection of water and other liquids, attest to the strong association of these objects with the primordial Goddess. Vases are also a symbol of life, with the liquid they hold—perhaps water—the elixir of life; in this tradition, the Chinese Kuan Yin holds a vase in one hand.

Signs and Symbols

Symbols can add another dimension and level of meaning to your altar, as well as to the rituals you perform in your sacred space. Using symbols with associations that reach far back in time connects us to all of our foremothers and forefathers and imbues our spirituality with a sense of time and history. Remember that you can incorporate symbols into your altar or sacred space in any number of ways. You can draw or sew the symbols you have chosen onto cloth or paper or use three-dimensional representations of a given symbol—a ring or a bracelet for a circle or a multicolored scarf for a rainbow, for example. Try rendering the symbol's shape using pebbles or rocks, seeds or beans, ribbons or strings of beads, or build your altar in a symbolic shape—setting it up as circular or triangular, or even incorporating the spokes of the wheel.

Symbols can also provide the focus for ritual and meditation. Use the symbol of the hand to promote healing or to focus on the importance of touch in your life; the depiction of a star or a star-shaped object can help you visualize ancestral spirits. Despite its seemingly ubiquitous commercial presence, the yin-yang symbol can provide the beginning for a meditation on finding balance in our lives amid what appear to be irreconcilable conflicts. By concentrating on the circle that contains dualities within, we can come to the understanding that "either or" is not always the answer and that the future may lie in the power of "and," symbolized by the circle that encloses the light and the dark, the masculine and the feminine. Spoked wheels and spirals, both emblems of rebirth and movement, can be incorporated into your altar as symbols of spiritual energy or can provide a starting place for a ritual about energy itself.

Lyda and Gerry—both of them self-described artisans who design for a creative outlet—built a round, portable altar out of wood, choosing pine for its simplicity and because the tree is a fast-growing one. Lyda then divided the circular form into twenty-six sections and burned twenty-five runic symbols into the wood, a process she describes as "becoming one with the wood, feeling its spirit," as meditative aids. Among the runes she used were those representing cooperation, partnership, health, home, mystery, restriction, completion, defense, protection, travel, fertility, possessions, joy, creativity, victory, intuition, prosperity, luck, reward, and wholeness; in the center, she left a blank space to represent karma, for which there is no symbol. On each of the runes, she placed a mineral or stone. Each morning, she chooses a rune from a bag, studies its meaning, and then takes the stone placed on the corresponding runic symbol on the altar for guidance. She carries it with her all day and replaces it in the evening, when she lights a white candle or incense at the center of the altar. (For more on runes, see page 73.)

Mundane objects can also be used on your altar to provide a focus for meditation and intention. Julie Middleton often deliberately places everyday things on her altar as another way "of integrating the mundane and spiritual lives"; in this context, a stapler can stand for connection and stability, a pen and paper for communication, a coin for financial concerns. Because her husband is a pilot, she always includes a small model of a plane.

Signs and symbols can be used in conjunction with colors, statuary, and animal guardians to focus the energy of your ritual space. Surround a figure of a goddess, for example, with spirals and triangles to exemplify her life-giving energy. Use the square, symbol of the terrestrial, in conjunction with gemstones and minerals that symbolize air and sky. An egg or egg-shaped object can bring the power of potential to your altar. Put a representation of a gate or door on your altar to signify passage, in conjunction with lunar symbols or with an animal guardian of change—the butterfly or frog, for example, or the bear for rebirth. Above all, feel free to create a personal vocabulary for your sacred space.

What follows is only a sampling of potent symbolism from cultures all over the world; for more, please consult Resources, page 204.

The ankh. The ancient Egyptians called it "the cross of life," "the key of life," or "the key of the Nile." Depicted in funerary art, the ankh is usually held by a god or goddess and signifies eternal life or resurrection. *See also the cross.*

The caduceus. A wand or staff with two entwined serpents, their heads facing each other, sometimes depicted with wings or a helmet, the caduceus has ancient roots and stands for fertility and life, wisdom and healing. In Sumer, it was a symbol of the goddess Inanna and her sacred marriage to Dumuzi, or Tammuz, as well as an emblem of the Tree of Life, as shown on the cup of Lagash from 2200 B.C.E. In ancient Greece, the caduceus belonged to Hermes, messenger of the gods and guider of souls; in his hands, it was a symbol of reconciliation and peace. Myth told how Hermes was given the staff by Apollo and how, upon finding two snakes fighting, Hermes pushed his staff between them. The caduceus was known to other cultures as well: in India, it appeared on stone tablets used as votive offerings at temples and in North America, on Aztec sacred art and in Native American painting. A confusion with the staff of Asclepius—a staff with a single snake wound around it—has also made the caduceus a symbol of healing and the medical profession.

The chakra. Taking its name from the Sanskrit word meaning "wheel" or "circle," the chakra was later associated with the disk of Vishnu, the solar deity and a symbol of the cosmic order; it found its way into Vedic, Jainist, Hindu, and Buddhist thought.

The circle. Perhaps the most important of all geometric symbols, the circle has long been thought to be the perfect form. The symbol of eternity, relation, unity, and equality, the circle has no beginning, no end, and no direction. It has been pictured in many ways: as a tied string by the ancient Egyptians or as a snake with its tail in its mouth by the Gnostics, among others. *(See the uroborus.)* Because we perceive the sun and the moon as circles in the sky, the circle also signified, for most cultures, the order of the cosmos. Thus, for most Native American peoples, the circle inscribed by the heavenly bodies provided the model for human activities, including seating, setting up camp, and dancing. The medicine wheel is perhaps the most important of the Native American circles.

As a fully enclosed form, the circle was thought to offer protection, as well as to mark a holy place. The caves of the Paleolithic, as well as the stone graves of the Neolithic, have circles and cup marks incised on them; the stone "circles" of England, Stonehenge among them, attest to the power of the shape, as do the circular holy places of the Druids and the circular Chinese Temple of Heaven. The god Shiva dances in a circle of fire representing the cosmos, and the "ring dances" of the fairies were thought to exercise a magic so powerful that anyone entering the circle would be instantly destroyed. Because rings and bracelets are circular, they symbolize wholeness and continuity; the magic powers often attributed to rings derive from their circularity as well. In Zen Buddhism, the circle represents enlightenment; the duality of yin and yang is enclosed in the oneness of the circle. In Christian symbolism, the circle represents God, who is both perfect and everlasting.

The four elements have also been depicted as circular in form: fire is a plain circle because of its weightlessness; a circle with a dot at its center denotes air; a circle with a marked diameter, water; and a circle with a cross at its center, divided into quarters, earth. In the Buddhist scheme of the five elements (earth, water, fire, air, ether), water is represented by a circle.

The cornucopia. The horn of abundance and a symbol of the bounties of nature often associated with rites of thanksgiving, the cornucopia derives some of its meaning from ancient associations with horns, sacred symbols of power and strength. In Greek myth, the original cornucopia belonged to the goat-shaped nymph Amalthea, who nursed Zeus as an infant on the island of Crete.

The cross. Though the cross has become primarily identified as a Christian symbol over the last two millennia, it is much older; it is worth remembering, too, that the early Church Fathers hesitated to adopt the cross as a symbol precisely because of its importance in pagan rituals. The shape of the cross suggests a still point or a place of intersection; it unifies the above and the below, the right and the left in its shape, which also echoes the form of the human body with outstretched arms. The Phoenicians associated the cross with the goddess Astarte, while the Greeks ascribed it to Artemis and Aphrodite. On the American continents, the Aztec goddess of the rains was associated with the cross, which may have symbolized either sun or wind; in Native American cultures, the cross signified the winds that bring the rains.

Because the cross has four parts, it has been associated as well with the four directions and the four elements. There are other important cruciform figures, among them:

Gammadian. Its name derived from its composition of four Greek gammas, the gammadian, a short-armed swastika, may have originally symbolized the four directions, or perhaps the two equinoxes and two solstices.

Swastika. Its name comes from two Sanskrit words (*su* for "good" and *asti* for "being"), meaning "it is well" or "so be it," and, long before it was debased as a Nazi emblem, the swastika was a sacred symbol in cultures all over the world; its crooked arms signified movement and energy, as well as generative power. It was associated with the four revolving seasons as well as the four directions, and it was the emblem of gods and goddesses alike. The swastika, along with the spiral, also stood for the turning bear constellation, Ursa Major, in the sky. The swastika is connected to both the sun and the moon; with arms moving clockwise, it is a solar symbol, and, with counterclockwise arms, lunar.

Lunate cross. With its four tips crowned by crescent moons facing outward, representing the phases of the moon, the lunate cross is a shamanic symbol.

Cross saltire, or Saint Andrew's cross. The tumbling cross saltire was thought to symbolize the union of the Upper and Lower Worlds. In the Vedas, it was a sign of the thunderbolt.

Tau cross. In the ancient Americas, the tau cross was called the "Tree of Life" or "Tree of Nutriment," and it was consecrated to the god of the rains. A bird is sometimes depicted on the fork of the cross. This symbol is also called "Thor's Hammer" and, in this context, is a symbol of rain, power, and fertility.

The cube. The three-dimensional rendering of the square, the cube represents the material world of the four elements and is associated with stability and permanence. In Revelation in the New Testament, the Heavenly Jerusalem is described as a cube.

The double ax. The sacred symbol of Minoan Crete, the *labrys,* or double ax, was probably a ritual instrument, which might once have been used for sacrifice; as a symbol, it stands for the Goddess's twinned powers of death and regeneration and is closely allied to the butterfly (see page 122).

The egg. A symbol with a rich and varied history, the egg and egg-shaped objects usually symbolize life, potentiality, and regeneration; in folklore, the egg often represents the seat of the soul. In Egyptian hieroglyphics, the egg stands for the seed of generation as well as the mystery of life. In many cultures, the Cosmic or World Egg, which yields the universe, forms the basis of creation myths. Eggs are also associated with magic and divination; the Romans crushed the shells of eggs they had eaten to destroy whatever magic was left in them.

The eye. The most vital sensory organ, the eye has long been associated with light and the sun and with intelligence and intuition, as well as the essence of truth that cannot be hidden. Statuary from third-millennium Sumer relates eye imagery to the feminine; known as "Eye goddesses," these statues were usually found in a funerary context and represent the feminine as the power of death. In ancient Egypt, the eye within the pyramid was the "Eye of Horus"; the eye represented the god's living spirit, waiting to be reborn. Precisely because the eye is associated with inner spirit, it has long been thought that malevolent creatures are able to cast "the evil eye" on unsuspecting victims.

The gate, the door, and the portal. The gate or door is an extremely powerful symbol that plays an extremely important part both in rituals and in the architecture of sacred spaces. The gate symbolizes passage, perhaps including a rite of passage, moving from one plane to another or from one stage to another. The door, too, symbolizes passage, although the closed door may also symbolize the mystery of knowledge to be attained.

Because doors and gates are protective, they separate both secular and sacred space from what is outside it; as a result, rituals, charms, and prayers dedicated to the parts of doorways—thresholds, lintels, and jambs—are prevalent the world over. In the Book of Exodus, the blood of the lamb was sprinkled on the doorposts of the Israelites so that God would keep those homes safe while he punished the Egyptians. Special deities protect doorways; in ancient Rome, the god Janus presided over the threshold, and his image was placed there. In Greece and Rome, Assyria, and Mexico, altars were placed near doorways, while splendid and often ornate gates, to which only high priestesses and priests held the keys, closed off the inner secret chambers of temples, known as the "holy of the holies." In Christianity, Christ identifies himself as "the door," while the Virgin Mary is the gateway to heaven.

The hand. Perhaps the oldest of all graphic symbols, the hand and the handprint have a multiplicity of meanings. The walls of many Paleolithic caves are decorated with silhouettes of hands as well as handprints made by dipping the hand in dye or paint, often in conjunction with other images and symbols (a pregnant mare, wavy lines represent-ing water, and crescent-shaped horns); they appear to signify the God-dess's energizing or life-giving touch. The appearance of handprints at the seventh-millennium shrines of Çatal Hüyük in Anatolia, along with other symbols (bullheads, bees, and butterflies) hints that the hand may symbolize becoming and generation. The power and magic of touch, symbolized by the hand, runs through many cultures; the hand can heal, bless, and confer power. In Egyptian hieroglyphics, the hand symbolizes action or manifestation; when the hand is combined with an eye, it means clairvoyant action. In Islamic cultures, the hand signifies protection, power, and strength, and it is often used as an amulet. The depiction of the Buddha's hand in imagery is also signifi-cant: see page 49.

The hexagram. Composed of two overlapping triangles, the hexa-gram, or six-pointed star, appears the world over. It is a symbol of du-ality enclosed by boundaries, for within it are the triangle pointing upward, associated with fire and the masculine, and the downward triangle, associated with water and the feminine. It has a long history as being magical in nature: Solomon was said to have summoned angels and banished demons with it. It is widely known as the Seal of Solomon, David's Shield, or the Star of David of Judaism. *See also the star.*

The key. A paradoxical emblem, long thought to have magical pow-ers, the key symbolizes both locking and unlocking, containment as well as setting free. The key often functions as a symbol of knowledge as well as of a task to be performed; in quests and journeys, finding a key is often the first step. Keys are associated with many gods and goddesses. Hecate was thought to hold the keys to the underworld and the universe, and a ritual dedicated to her was called "the proces-sion of the keys." The key to Athens was in Athena's hand, while the Egyptian Serapis held the keys to earth and sea. In Babylonian myth,

Marduk manufactured the keys to heaven and hell; Ishtar could open them. In the New Testament, Jesus gives Peter the keys to the kingdom of heaven.

Because of their magical power, keys were used as amulets to lock out and ward off evil spirits and demons. They were also used to "lock in" beneficial occurrences or to effect a release: keys to a sacred place were put under the heads of the dying to release them from the pangs of death. In Roman times, keys were given to women in labor to facilitate birth.

The knot. While a knot is an emblem of unity and bonding, connected to the symbolism of weaving, the symbolism of untying the knot is equally potent as a release of energy. The image of the woven web of life is pervasive in ancient cultures from the three Fates of the Greeks to the Germanic Norns. In ancient Egypt, Isis tied and loosed the knot of life, and holy mysteries were known as "she-knots"; the knot secured the circle of eternity, the loop of the ankh, and the cartouche around the sacred name of a pharaoh. The Egyptian goddesses Hathor and Isis also wore a *menat*, a knotted headband or necklace. According to Anne Baring and Jules Cashford, in ancient Crete a knot of hair, cloth, or grain hung at the entrance to a shrine indicated the presence of the Goddess, as representations of sacred knots engraved on gems and in stone make clear. In Chinese Buddhism, the "endless knot" is a symbol of longevity and one of the eight emblems of good luck.

The knot, though, could also be an impediment: for the Romans, the sacred precinct of the goddess of childbirth, Juno Lacinia, was forbidden to anyone wearing a knotted or tied garment because "knots" impede delivery. The idea of the knot as binding or fettering the spirit is present as well in the injunction against Muslims' having knots on their pilgrimages to Mecca. Knots were also once associated with witchcraft and magic; thus, Jews were forbidden by rabbinical law to tie knots on the Sabbath.

The mystical symbolism of the knot is perhaps best exemplified by the Gordian knot, for whoever could unravel it would rule all of Asia. It symbolized a journey to the center of meaning, much like the thread that leads into the center of the labyrinth. The ever-pragmatic Alexander the Great, not big on mysticism, simply cut the Gordian knot with his sword.

Actual knots, as well as intricate knotwork patterns drawn on paper, can be used on your altar to release energy as well as to signify commitment, still evident in the expression we use for marriage: "tying the knot."

The labyrinth. While it takes its name from the *labrys,* or the sacred double ax of ancient Crete, the labyrinth and its symbolism are, in fact, much older. Labyrinthine designs are incised on the walls of Paleolithic caves, and it seems possible that the sacred caves humanity first worshiped in, which required crawling through narrow passages and over dangerous precipices to the cave's ritual center, were the model for the labyrinth. The labyrinth represents a journey to the center, a return to the beginning through darkness that ends in rebirth.

You can incorporate a labyrinthine design on your altar by using rocks or beads or simply drawing one on paper. For more on the labyrinth, see "The Labyrinth: A Spiritual Path," page 180.

The ladder. In Judeo-Christian traditions, the ladder is a symbol of the link between earth and heaven, the world of the spirit and the world of corporeality, as it is in other cultures. In ancient Egypt, the "ladder" (or the staircase) was a symbol of the sun god; small ladder amulets were left in the tombs of kings to facilitate their access to the realm of the gods. Most important of the ladders mentioned in the Bible is Jacob's ladder, which reached from earth to heaven and presaged God's address to Jacob; angels ascended and descended on it. Elsewhere, the ladder stands for the trances of shamans, the "ladders" that elevate them above the plane of life.

This meditation shelf set upon a molding only a few inches deep in Peter's apartment reminds us that the creation of sacred space does not require a mansion; each of the objects on the shelf is small, the tallest of them no more than three or four inches high. Exquisite in its simplicity, a painted Buddha hangs over the shelf, along which the owner has arranged gifts and offerings that are more personal than traditional. The rock with a natural spiral of a different color is there for movement and change, as are the shells brought to shore by the ocean's currents. Next to the small vase filled with dried wheat sits a pocket-size Buddha carved out of crystal for clarity and an owl for wisdom. Only the showy blossoms of the hibiscus in a vase with a small pineapple for hospitality seem to break the quiet of this space.

The mandorla. From the Italian for "almond," the mandorla is now primarily a Christian symbol of divinity, an almond-shaped aureole that, in paintings, encloses either Christ or the Virgin Mary. It does, however, have more ancient roots. Because its shape suggests a schematized vulva, it is often a symbol of the feminine. On the other hand, because the almond was a symbol of a hard shell enclosing something valuable within, it is also an emblem of treasure.

The obelisk. Mainly associated with the ancient Egyptians, obelisks, which are slender, four-sided, tapering monuments ranging in height from three to hundreds of feet, were dedicated to the sun god and stood alongside the doors of temples as well as tombs. Though they are primarily associated with the phallic and the masculine, it is worth noting that the temple of Astarte at Byblos was flanked by a tall stone, or obelisk.

The pentacle, or pentagram. Although the five-pointed star is now primarily associated with magic and witchcraft, the pentacle, along with other geometric figures with five parts, was once a symbol of the feminine and the Earth Mother. The apple, once a sacred fruit, yields a pentacle at its core when it is cut on the transverse. In Egyptian hieroglyphics, the pentacle denoted elucidation; it meant, variously, "to educate" or "to rise up" or "to bring up." For the Gnostics, for whom the number five was sacred, the pentacle was an important symbol; for the Pythagoreans, the pentacle stood for the harmony of the body and the mind and was therefore a symbol of health. The pentacle had such sacred roots that it even became a Christian symbol: its five points stood for the five wounds Christ suffered on the cross; its interconnected lines denoted the alpha and omega, the first and last, of Christ. A single star was traditionally a symbol of the Virgin Mary as Stella Maris, or "Star of the Sea."

The pentagram's association with magic—both black and white—has overpowered the other meanings it once had; with its point up, it is a symbol of white magic and, with its point down, of black. As such, the pentacle was often inscribed on doors and doorways to keep demons away. See also "Numbers," page 78.

The pyramid. Like the triangle, the pyramid symbolizes the earth in its maternal aspect and is a feminine symbol.

The rainbow. Not surprisingly, in many cultures, the rainbow symbolizes the connection between earth and sky, the mundane and the divine. It is also a symbol of communication: just as the Greek goddess of the rainbow, Iris, carried messages from the gods to the mortals below, so too, in the Old Testament, after the floodwaters had receded, the rainbow appeared to Noah as a symbol of God's continued favor. In Norse myth, the rainbow was the bridge between earth and Valhalla, guarded by Heimdall. The accessibility of the rainbow as a path to the heavenly realm was, though, also considered to be a matter of goodness or virtue. The many colors of the rainbow are connected to the veils of Maya and those of Ishtar as well; in this context, the rainbow stands for the multiplicity contained in the world. In Native America, the rainbow had a number of different associations. For the Tlingit, it was the road of the dead, while the Pueblo Indians and the Navajo recognized it as the road by which the spirits and the gods traveled. In other Native American myths, the rainbow is also a bridge of the spirit, connecting this world to another. Contemporary usage recognizes the rainbow as a symbol of diversity within oneness.

The rune. In early Anglo-Saxon, "rune" means "mystery" or "secret," and it would seem these symbolic markings, once thought to be linked to the powers of magic held by specific gods, were used as oracles and tools of divination as early as the first century throughout northern Europe, England, Ireland, and Scotland. There are two runic alphabets, one of sixteen characters and one of twenty-four.

In Norse myth, the goddess Idun, the Ever-Renewing One because she guarded the apples of immortality, was said to have invented runes.

The spiral. Along with the triangle, the spiral is the symbol most closely allied with the feminine. Its dynamic shape suggests energy unfolding and is closely allied to the snake (see page 134); alternating spirals, moving upward and downward, are also connected to lunar cycles. Since the Paleolithic, spiral forms have been incised and drawn on sacred places and objects, symbolizing the Goddess and her awesome powers of death and rebirth; in this context, a spiral within a triangle suggests the feminine energy of life. In the Cyclades, spirals were drawn on walls and rocks that probably served as outdoor altars; they also appear in every cemetery as a symbol of regeneration.

The square. The opposite of the circle, the square represents order as well as direction; it is terrestrial in nature and finite, in contrast to the eternal nature of the circle. In the Chinese and Hindu traditions, the square is identified as feminine in nature because of its connection to the earth. If, as Carl Jung reasoned, the circle is the symbol of oneness, then the square symbolizes the human state when inner unity has not yet been achieved. In contrast, in Egyptian hieroglyphics, the square denotes achievement. Like the circle, the square has served as the geometric model for sacred places: the Kaaba ("Cube") shrine at Mecca, the primary pilgrimage for Muslims, is a cube. See also "Mandala," page 96.

The star. In the broadest sense, the star is a symbol of the cosmic order, for the stars above us revolve on a fixed path around the polestar. In many traditions, the star represents the heavenly presence of the dead; the Jewish cosmological tradition held that each star had a guardian angel, while the Aztecs saw the star as the manifested spirit of a sacrificed or fallen warrior. The star is also a symbol of the spirit that shines despite the surrounding forces of darkness.

In Greek myth, the Milky Way was created while the goddess Hera nursed the infant Hercules; when she pulled her breast away, the milk spilled over into the night sky, making the Milky Way.

The triangle. The most powerful and the earliest of the symbols pertaining to the feminine, the triangle symbolizes the generative power of the female, inspired by the shape of the vulva. In the Paleolithic, skulls were buried under triangular rocks to invoke the Goddess's power of rebirth. For the Pythagoreans, the Greek letter delta—a triangle—signified cosmic birth; in Hinduism, the triangle stands for the goddess Durga. Triangles pointing down are water symbols; when they point upward, they signify fire.

The triangle was also a symbol of the triple Goddess—maiden, mother, and crone; in later Christian symbolism, the triangle stood for the Trinity of Father, Son, and Holy Ghost.

The uroborus. The image of the snake biting its own tail, the uroborus, is an ancient symbol of the cyclical nature of life and the universe, as well as of death and rebirth. Found in ancient Egypt, China, as well as European cultures, it is also a powerful emblem of the eternal.

The wheel. Though the wheel is closely related to the circle, nonetheless its spokes signify meaningful differences. If the circle is immutable, then the wheel implies change, movement, and becoming. For the Romans, the wheel became the symbol of life, or the attribute of the goddess Fortuna, who ruled over the changes in the fortunes of each human being, an image that would, eventually, make its way into the tarot deck as the Wheel of Fortune. Because the sun appears to move through the sky and is pictured in many cultures as a chariot, the wheel has many solar associations. Solstice celebrations were often marked by rolling flaming wheels down hills. The wheel is a positive symbol as the emblem of rebirth. In Buddhism, the wheel—known variously as the Wheel of Life, Wheel of Truth, the Holy Wheel, the Wheel of the Law, or the Wheel of a Thousand Spokes—is an elaborate and inspiring emblem. First and foremost, it symbolizes the effect of Buddha's wisdom on delusion and falsehood, crushing what came before as the wheel flattens what lies in its path. Buddha himself is said to have fashioned the design with grains of rice plucked from a stalk as he taught his disciples. The spokes of the Wheel correspond to the rules of conduct Buddha taught, as well as to the sacred rays of light that emanated from him. See also "Prayer Wheels," page 99.

Wings. The depiction of gods and goddesses as winged is ancient, and probably derives from even older levels of meaning associated with the wings of the birds; wings symbolize thought, imagination, and spirit and suggest a higher level of attainment and intensity. Thus, the power of the horse with wings, Pegasus, becomes a symbol of the imaginative flight of poetry.

The yin and yang. Once solely a feminine symbol related to the lunar calendar, the yin and yang evolved as the circle divided by an **S**-curve, half white and half black. Each side is punctuated by a small circle of the opposite color, signifying that each of a pair of opposites contains something of the other in its nature. Together, the yin (the feminine) and the yang (the masculine) constitute perfect balance.

....

A sense of the sacred can be integrated into your work space in many different ways. In more formal, corporate settings, a grouping of objects with personal resonance and meaning can provide you with a place of quiet, where, in the course of a hectic working day, you can take a deep inner breath. Particularly if you work in an ultramodern building where you are literally cut off from the natural world by air-conditioning and permanently closed windows, try bringing in something that reminds you of life's beauty; even a single flower in the smallest of vases can serve as a mandala, or focal point. This altar in a home office setting, described fully on pages 28-29, acts as visual reminder of all the sources of inspiration in the owner's life.

Numbers

We have no way of knowing when humanity first perceived numbers as sacred symbols of the supernatural, mystical and symbolic of numinous power, but we do know that it was very early in human history. Observing the natural world, particularly the cycles of the moon, probably first prompted an understanding of numerical patterns. The red-painted figure of a woman, carved over 20,000 years ago in a rock shelter at Laussel in the Dordogne region of France, once graced a place of ritual that looked over a valley. In the woman's left hand, she holds a horn carved in the shape of a crescent moon; on it are thirteen notches. Her right hand rests on her belly, swollen with pregnancy. The number thirteen—the number of the lunar months in a yearly cycle—provides the connection between the celestial pattern and the earthly one of blood and birth. Thirteen, now considered an unlucky number, was once the number of life.

Through the millennia, humanity has continued to see numbers as signposts of divine order, indicative of the spirit behind physical reality. Among the Greeks and Romans, the numbers 3, 9, and 12 had magical significance, while in ancient China, the numbers 5 and 8 organized the universe. There were five points of the compass, five colors, five forms of earthly happiness, five viscera, five tastes, and five pure things, all of them ruled by the five elements. There were eight trigrams connected to the points of the compass, eight immortals, eight treasures, eight auspicious signs, and eight ordinary symbols.

Each culture has its own vision of number and meaning incorporated into belief and rite, but, in the West, no philosophy has had greater influence on the understanding of the importance of number than Pythagoras. Born in the sixth century B.C.E., Pythagoras studied with the temple priests of ancient Egypt before returning to his homeland, Greece. There, he and his disciples preached a discipline that saw number as the essence of all things—all matter, all ethical and moral concepts, all thought. Pythagoras and his followers believed that "all things are number," and that the universe was a union of opposites, each symbolized by number, which included limited and unlimited, odd and even, right and left, male and female, rest and motion, straight and curved, light and dark, and good and evil. In addition to the immortality of the soul, they also believed in the blood-brotherhood of men and beasts and thus taught respect for animals. In order to free their souls from the "wheel of life," they followed strict rules of purification, moral codes, and dietary practices. In addition to their contributions to the sciences of astronomy and medicine and to Euclidean geometry, they also bequeathed an influential and mystical vision of number.

Numbers can be used on your altar along with other symbolism. One woman I know built a relationship altar that was entirely composed of twos or pairs—two candles, two stones, two incense burners, two shells—so that she could focus on the meaning of the dyad. Numbers can be used consciously, or you can let them reveal themselves.

One. One is often the number of the deity, the divine or the creative principle; in ancient Egypt, Ra was worshiped as "the one One." For the Pythagoreans, one was the immutable number, symbol of Thought, indivisible. It was the Divine Monad from which all else flowed.

Two. Two is, first and foremost, the number of relationship and pairing. In the Paleolithic and Neolithic, Marija Gimbutas has suggested, double images signified the potency and abundance of the feminine life force. Two may also stand for equilibrium, as well as the continuum of life, which includes life and death; it was a symbol of the Magna Mater, or Great Mother. Two can also be used as the number of dualism, either resolved or in conflict; it can stand for linked contraries, such as day and night, light and dark, love and hatred. The Pythagoreans understoond it as the first female number, identified with "opinion."

Three. Perceived as one of the most mystical of numbers in many cultures, the number three symbolizes the beginning, middle, and end and the cycle of life: birth, growth, and death. It is also associated with the feminine in mythology the world over. The Goddess was, for thousands of years, honored in her three aspects: as a young maiden, as a mother, and as an old woman endowed with wisdom. The Greeks associated the triple goddess with Hecate, the three-faced moon goddess, who presided over the *tri via,* or crossroads. The triple goddess was associated with the life force and death as well as the three realms: she was Selene, the moon in the heavens; Artemis, the huntress on earth; and Persephone presiding over the underworld. Threesomes of female divinities seem to underscore their power and influence. Because nine is the square of three, even the nine Greek Muses were essentially triadic in nature. For the Pythagoreans, three was the symbol of cosmic order: the synthesis of one and two.

In China, three is the perfect number, and in Buddhism, fulfillment is found in the Triple Jewel.

Four. Inextricably linked to the square and the cube, the number four is associated with the solid as well as the earthly; there are four directions, four quarters of earth, four phases of the moon, and four seasons. In ancient Egypt, the number four was the number of completion. The Pythagoreans regarded four as the number of earth, material, and substance. In many Native American ceremonies, four is the number of completion.

Five. For the Pythagoreans, five was a number of great mystical significance, representing the marriage of the numbers two and three, of Earth and Heaven, of female and male, respectively. Five is also a potent magical number that, when represented in the five-pointed pentacle, can provide great protection. Among the Aztecs, the dead were reborn on the fifth day.

Six. For the Greeks, six was Aphrodite's number, the number of love and completion. In China, six is the number of Heaven; in the Old Testament, there were six days of creation.

Seven. According to the Pythagoreans, seven was the most holy and sacred of numbers; in Greece, the seventh day was sacred to Apollo. Revered among the Persians, Sumerians, Egyptians (who understood seven to be the number of eternal life), Assyrians, and Teutonic tribes, seven appears with mystical significance in the Old Testament as well. In Joshua, seven priests with seven ram's horns circled the walls of Jericho for seven days. On the seventh day, they circled the walls seven times, and the walls fell. In the Middle Ages, the altar of a church was decorated with seven precious or semiprecious stones: diamond or crystal for strength, a sapphire or other blue stone for wisdom, an emerald or green stone for skill in change, a topaz for knowledge, a jasper for beauty, a red stone—a ruby, a carnelian, or a garnet—for devotion, and an amethyst for prayer.

Each phase of the moon lasts seven days; the four together equal twenty-eight (7 times 4), as does the sum of the first seven numbers (1 plus 2 plus 3 plus 4 plus 5 plus 6 plus 7). Among the Plains Indians, seven was the number of the cosmic coordinates (the four directions, the top and bottom of the vertical axis, and the center).

Eight. Eight is, among many peoples, the number of cosmic balance. The Buddhist Wheel of Law has eight spokes, the lotus has eight petals, and there are eight trigrams in the *I Ching*. For the Greeks, eight is the number of the Earth Mother and other goddesses; the

Parthenon, dedicated to Athena, had eight columns in the front as the goddess's sacral number.

Nine. As the number three squared, nine is the number of a higher power, associated in ancient Egypt with the powerful grouping of nine gods known as an ennead.

Ten. Traditionally, ten is the number of completion, probably for the simple reason that counting began on fingers, of which there are ten. Among the Pythagoreans, it was the holiest of all numbers and a symbol, as well, on which they took their oaths, for the sum of the first four numbers (1 plus 2 plus 3 plus 4) equals ten. As a symbol, the Sacred Tetractys was composed of ten dots arranged in a pyramid with each successive level below it:

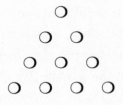

The single dot was the principle of all things, or the Monad or godhead; the second, the dyadic in all things; the third, the levels of the world; the fourth, the earth and the entire physical world; and the figure as a whole, the entire universe, created and uncreated.

Altar Building as a Creative Process

This is a place where you can simply experience and bring forth what you are and what you might be. This is the place of creative incubation. At first you may find nothing happens there. But if you have a sacred place and use it, something eventually will happen.

JOSEPH CAMPBELL
on having a sacred place, from *The Power of Myth*

The word *create* is from the Latin, and it means "to bring into being or existence." Altar building is a creative process precisely because it brings into being—that is, into physical form—the feelings and thoughts that are within us. As you choose the place in your home or garden to establish your sacred space, listen to the voice within: Will you be comfortable here? What does this piece of your home or garden actually feel like to you? What kind of associations does it bring forth?

Listening to yourself is an important part, too, of choosing the objects for your altar. *Don't* build your altar with the same need to rush and perform that might dominate the rest of your life; permit yourself the time to visualize your sacred space and to decide what *you* need in it. Think about what is important or meaningful to you at this time in your life.

Your sacred space will be a place where, in Campbell's words, "you can experience who you are and who you might be." By experiencing the self fully, we are able to transcend the self and its everyday rhythms and needs as well as the demands the outside world places on it. Create a space where you can come into contact with all that lies within the self and all that lies outside it.

The words of Walt Whitman, too, remind us to slow down and listen:

> This thy hour O soul, thy free flight into the wordless,
> Away from books, away from art, the day erased, the lesson
> done,
> Thee fully forth emerging, silent, gazing, pondering . . .

2

Energizing Sacred Space

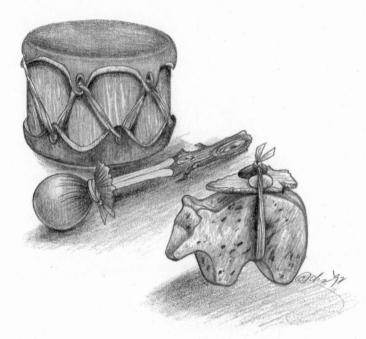

Kindling the Spirit

How you use your sacred space and the role it plays in your daily life is, of course, a completely individual matter, and, not surprisingly, there are significant differences in how people approach energizing sacred space. Many people follow strict rituals in cleansing their space—smudging or rededicating their altars with ceremonies at specific times (at the equinoxes and solstices and cross-quarters of the year, for example), with smoke and water, by lighting incense, by drumming or ringing bells. Some change what they do each time they approach their altar, depending on why they have come to their sacred space: to seek solace or help, to celebrate or to mark a transition, or to meditate or pray. Others, some of whom have now been building altars for well over a decade, find that their practices have shifted as their spiritual vocabulary has grown, beginning with formal rites of smudging and cleansing and ending with simple prayers or invocations. Nancy Blair has grown away from the practice, for she dislikes the negative premise of the altar's being somehow dirty or defiled; she uses words and images to release any unhealthy energy. Others assert that it is preparation of the altar itself that matters, and that the intention built up during the altar's creation is sufficient to energize it. Sarah Teofanov, for example, no longer goes through a formal process of cleansing, because she uses the materials for her altars over and over again, set apart from mundane objects in her life; in her words, energizing her sacred space is simply a matter of "bringing the respect to the altar that it deserves."

Perhaps the most compelling reason to consciously reenergize your sacred space has more to do with you than the space itself. Incorporating ritual gestures—smudging or burning incense, drumming, bell ringing, or chanting—into the use of sacred space helps many people shed their everyday concerns—the unanswered phone call, the business connection missed, the demands of children—and permits them to focus instead on the spiritual work they need to do. These gestures have the added advantage of cleansing, of freeing up, the self. They make it possible for a person to create what Brooke Medicine Eagle, in her book *Buffalo Woman Comes Singing*, has called the "necklace of connectedness."

Cleansing and, sometimes, dismantling an altar that has been built for a specific purpose can also provide a sense of closure. On her altar (described on page 16), Cindy would also leave cards with words or pictures describing her wishes and aspirations; they were there, she says, to remind her that, in addition to intentions, actions were also important. At the end of each quarter, when she cleansed her altar, she burned these cards—to release her aspirations to the larger world and to permit her to move on. When an altar is no longer useful or pertinent to Julie Middleton, she lights a candle, thanks it for its help, and then clears off the altar down to the bare wood. She then begins the altar building process anew.

The pages that follow present ways of energizing both your altar and your rituals. Once again, I would encourage you to follow your own path and to use these as suggestions rather than as a blueprint.

Water

The essence and preserver of life, the primordial fluid on which birth and growth depend, water has always been recognized as sacral. It has long been used to purify, to energize, to heal, and to consecrate. Early on in human history, the energy of flowing water was identified with the life force itself, and, not surprisingly, the earliest of Paleolithic sanctuaries are located near sacred rivers and springs, as many of humanity's most sacred places of pilgrimage continue to be. Zigzags and meanders, which Marija Gimbutas has identified as emblematic of water and life, adorned both sacral objects and edifices. The cup marks—small, round indentations in rock and stone—that decorate sacred places from their earliest beginnings were probably used to collect the water that fell from the sky. Vessels from the Neolithic, deliberately perforated with holes, make it clear that collecting and then sprinkling rainwater for the sympathetic magic is an ancient practice. Lustral basins for rites of purification stood at the entrances of Minoan shrines, as they did at the temples of Malta, Greece, and Rome, and as they continue to do in holy places the world over.

In addition to being used as an offering (see page 146) or in conjunction with *feng shui* (page 22), water can also energize you and your sacred space. Scent the water, if you wish, using herbs, flower petals, or simply a bit of lemon peel, and wash your hands and face as an act of purification; you may want to sprinkle some of the water on the objects on your altar as well. Some people collect rainwater to use on their altars, while others believe that letting water stand either in the full rays of the sun or in the light of the moon will give it energy.

Another way of energizing your sacred space is simply to meditate on water itself, remembering that we ourselves are largely made up of water. If we can visualize the water within us, we can ally ourselves with the streams, rivers, and oceans and all of their life forms, as well as the tides pulled by the moon. Absorb the understanding that everything we know as living begins in water: without water, nothing living on the planet as we know it would exist. If you need added energy, visualize the water as coursing and rushing, smoothing the rocks and stones in its path; if you need to relax, imagine the stillness of a pond, its waters dappled by sunlight.

Fire, Light, and Smoke

Humanity's earliest rites conducted in the subterranean vaults of the earth involved the use of light—hollowed out lamps of stone with bits of burning moss floating in fat—and so, in all parts of our planet, the sacred continues to be celebrated, as it always has, with light and fire. The symbolism of bringing light to darkness, of awakening and illuminating in literal and metaphoric ways, is universal. On contemporary altars—regardless of the rite or system of beliefs honored at each sacred space—candles burn brightly, just as, in centuries past, torch- or candlelit processions invigorated and purified the fields ready for sowing, and honored or propitiated the spirits. All over the world, too, candles are lit and fires stoked in commemoration of the dead.

Some people place candles on their altars to invite the deity in or as an offering to the deity; others, like Julie Middleton, use different candles to symbolize different prayers. She chooses both different shapes and colors of candles: green or brown for the earth, white or yellow for air, orange or red for fire, blue or purple for water, and pink or red for love.

The bright flame of a candle can also be used as the focus for meditation. Because of their mythic origin in the divine, fire and flame, as well as smoke, have long been thought to bridge the space between heaven and earth, here and there.

Please remember *never* to leave a candle or fire unattended and to make sure that your candle rests on a fireproof surface. Make sure, too, that the candle is placed far enough away from anything that might possibly catch fire. If you are moving around your altar (drumming or dancing, for example), make sure *nothing*—including clothing and hanging hair—can fly into the flame.

Most of the symbolism connected to fire, light, and smoke is familiar, but remembering the meaning of the lighted candle gives new energy and spirit to the gesture.

For information on smudging, please see "Herbs and Spices," page 154 and following.

Fire. Mythology puts us in touch with how vital fire was to humanity's understanding of the sacral, for, in most of the world's myths, fire is depicted as stolen from the gods, often by a trickster figure, and given to humanity. Closely allied to the power of the sun, fire symbolizes heat, passion, and the life force. Fire was one of the four elements of the ancients in the West, and one of the five elements of the Chinese. To look into a fireplace puts us instantly in touch with why fire was always perceived as a living being, full of power and magic as well as contradiction. Fire is both destructive and consuming, connected to lust and passion; yet it is also purifying, emblematic of warmth, illumination, and love. The ritual fires of Beltane and Midsummer were purifying and regenerative, imitating the sun's rebirth in the sky each morning.

Fire, too, is a part of the sacrality of the hearth, center of the home, marriage, and the community; divine in origin, it symbolizes continuity and inspiration, as well as civilization. Symbol of sunlight, fire also stands for new beginnings and regeneration, so the candle becomes a signpost to the future. The flame too signifies eternality.

Light. Symbolic of goodness and knowledge as well as the spirit, light finds its opposite in darkness, with which, in most creation myths, it was once one; the separation of light and dark is the primary act of creation. In the Christian tradition, a halo is simply a reflection of the goodness or light within, while, in Buddhism, the whole universe blazed with light when the Buddha reached the perfection of knowledge.

Smoke. Trailing wisps of smoke spiraling up into the air have been understood by many cultures as a direct way of communicating with the spirits of the heavens, taking prayers and blessings to them; the smoke that curled from the resins lit by the ancient Egyptians carried their prayers, as it would for untold numbers of others with different spiritual beliefs. Among the Native Americans, smoke unified earth and sky and symbolized the true spirit within; it purified as well when obtained by smudging, the ritual burning of grasses or herbs. See also "Tobacco," page 146.

The Power of Scent

The use of incense—originally burned gums or resins—in religious ceremonies is universal and ancient in its origins. Though incense was used for its fumigatory and cleansing power, it also played, as it continues to, an important symbolic role in ritual observance. The perfume released by the incense symbolized the active presence of a higher spirit, god, or goddess, while the smoke wafting up from the incense represented prayers, thus bridging the gap between the earthly and the spiritual. Scent affected the worshipers as well, since it has long been known that scents have the ability to influence how we feel—calming or agitating, evoking thought and memory—and think. As did all of the generations before us, each of us has deep-seated associations with scent and smell, and many people find that burning incense readies their spirit as they prepare to pray or meditate.

The ancient Egyptians used incense in a censer as an offering, and images show worshipers with a libation or other gift in one hand and a censer in the other. They worshiped Ra, the sun god, by burning resin at sunrise, myrrh at midday, and, at sunset, a special incense called *kupki,* a mixture of sixteen ingredients, including honey, wine, raisins, myrrh, and sweet calamus. The preparation of *kupki* was itself a sacral activity, for holy writings were read to the preparers as they worked. According to Plutarch, the sweet smell of *kupki* both propitiated the gods and soothed the spirits of the worshipers. The cubes of incense were kept in a vessel in the shape of a hawk's head crowned by a solar disk in honor of Ra. The burning incense, too, symbolized the purification of the soul by prayer, as it would in many other systems of belief.

The ancient Greeks burned incense at the temples of the gods and goddesses, while in Rome, incense burning was a part of both public ritual and private rites at home, honoring the *lars familaris,* or spirit of the home. The Old Testament provides very explicit instructions about incense, its burning on the altar, and its consecration to God in the books of Exodus and Leviticus; the early Christians used incense in the catacombs, and by the fifth century, the use of incense in Christian worship was established, although, perhaps because of the strong association of incense with pagan religions, Clement of Alexandria averred, "The true altar of incense is the just soul, and the perfume from it holy prayer."

The sweetness of incense, too, plays a part in its meaningfulness. In Buddhism, the fragrance of the incense symbolizes the sweetness of Buddha's teachings, which, like the scent, permeates all around it; a blessing is said when the incense is lit. In Hinduism, *tulsi,* or holy basil, is consecrated to Vishnu and Krishna and is either burned as an offering or worshiped in plant form.

Contemporary interest in aromatherapy has also opened up many people's understanding of the use of scents to revitalize, stimulate, or calm the spirit. A few drops of essential oil added to a bowl of nearly boiling water can clear your sacred space, as can misting with a diffuser that has a few drops of essential oil added to it. Different oils have different effects, so, once again, your choice should depend on your own needs. For invigoration and uplift, try spearmint or peppermint, lime or lemon, or rosemary. To soothe the spirit, try floral scents such as rose or lavender or ylang-ylang. For cleansing, use sage, thyme, or pine. For the quiet meditative spirit, use sandalwood, frankincense, or cedarwood.

Whether you decide to use incense or essential oils to purify or cleanse your sacred space or simply to create an atmosphere hospitable to prayer and meditation is a matter of personal choice. Try choosing a scent that isn't overpowering so it does not itself become a distraction. Choosing a scent is a highly personal matter; I can't bear the smell of sandalwood, for example, while the floral scents I prefer are considered heavy by many people I know.

Last, though hardly least, is the fragrance of flowers. During the winter months on the East Coast, when night falls early and it is often too cold to really enjoy the outdoors, I find that the scent of fresh flowers is an instant spiritual tonic. If you are lucky enough to have a garden or access to fresh flowers, nothing will energize your sacred space more than the lush, sweet smell of a freshly cut rose or the morning sweetness of meadow flowers. An added bonus is the flower's beauty.

Tools for Prayer and Meditation

Creating an altar or sacred space is the first part of the journey; readying ourselves to be a part of it is the next. For many people in these contemporary times, "readying" is actually closer to a process of "undoing" or "unplugging" all the wires and buttons that keep us moving throughout our busy quotidian lives—the quick gesture to pick up a ringing phone, the mental notes not to forget the dry cleaning or the bread for dinner, the hurried glance at the clock to make sure we haven't somehow managed to forget a child at soccer practice or left a client waiting.

This isn't a new problem, of course. Though we certainly have more ringing and clanging pieces of electronic and other equipment than our ancestors did, nonetheless, concentrating and clarifying the mind for meditation and prayer has always required effort. There are many different ways of "readying" the mind—by deep breathing and relaxation, by the use of sound or music, by concentration on a symbolic object (such as a mandala or, like the medieval monks, a flower laden with symbolism), by recitation of a word or words, by using a rosary, by focusing on a representation of a deity, or by visualizing a feeling or thought.

Following are some of the "tools" from different cultures that you might want to incorporate into your own process of "readying" as you create your altar or sacred space:

Mandala. From the Sanskrit for "circle," in Tibetan Buddhism the mandala is a concentric diagram meant as an aid to meditation and enlightenment; it is composed of circles and other geometric figures. It is a graphic representation of the cosmic forces, or the world order. A mandala can be drawn or painted or can be rendered in three dimensions; it can also be represented by heaps of rice or drawn with colored sand. Because mandalas appear in sacred art the world over, Carl Jung identified the mandala as an archetype, the four corners of which symbolize the world or cosmos, both within and without. In his book *The Power of Myth,* Joseph Campbell suggests that you make your own mandala, beginning by drawing a circle and composing a scheme of all "the different impulse systems and value systems in your life." As he puts it, "Making a mandala is a discipline for pulling all those scattered aspects of your life together, for finding a center and ordering yourself to it."

Mantra. Ritual words and phrases, or mantras, are considered to be the sound form of reality representing the cosmic forces; they manifest the energy of the cosmos and therefore are capable of bringing that energy into reality. A mantra is used as a form of meditation to render the mind spiritually receptive and connect the person saying it to the vibrations of the universe. In Tibetan Buddhism, the oldest and most important mantra is *Om Mani Padme Hum,* or "Om, Jewel in the Lotus, Hum." It can be written and then visualized, either within the body of the meditator or outside it, or it can be spoken. Protective mantras—either invoking the aid of a benevolent deity, such as the Green Tara, or protection against a potentially malevolent one—are often said in conjunction with a rosary or *mala.*

Medicine bundle. From the Native American tradition, a medicine bundle is a collection of sacred or magical objects, usually wrapped in skin, that is thought either to have been bestowed by supernaturals or assembled according to their instructions. Used in all manner of rite and ceremony, medicine bundles can be personal, belonging to the individual, or the property of a tribe. The medicine bundle is considered to be of great power and is assembled with ritual care with specifically chosen objects before each ceremony. In certain tribes, the medicine bundle of an individual is ritually disposed of after the owner's death. You can make your own medicine bundle, which might include both objects that are generally considered sacred and those that are of purely personal significance. In her book *Buffalo Woman Comes Singing,* Brooke Medicine Eagle suggests creating a medicine bundle that stands for an important vision and using the medicine bundle, either on your altar or elsewhere, to help you visualize it. In the same way, you could create a medicine bundle for meditative purposes or to help you visualize and actualize a spiritual or emotional goal.

Prayer flags. In the Tibetan tradition, motion supplied by the winds sends written prayers into the ether (the element associated with the deities) to the ears of the supernaturals. Traditionally, there are five different types of prayer flags, with each color connected to a different element: red to earth, green to water, yellow to fire, blue to air, and white to ether.

Many people I have spoken to have adapted the idea of the prayer flag in wonderful ways, making their own out of fabric or paper, writing prayers and intentions on them, and incorporating them into rituals. They can be used for both indoor and outdoor altars.

Prayer sticks. Among the Southwestern tribes of Native America, a prayer stick is an implement invoking supernatural aid. Although the prayer stick is often a stick with feathers, the word *ke-tan* in Navajo means "place-where-it-is-feathered"; according to Gladys Reichard, the word may also encompass other ceremonial objects that have the same power of invocation. A prayer stick functions on a number of levels: as protection for the individual who carries it; as an offering; as a messenger or conveyor of the prayer or invocation to the deities; or as a symbolic prayer in and of itself. In the latter case, the elements of which the prayer stick is made (different feathers, beads, gems, colors) actually stand for the words or phrases of the chant or prayer to be spoken and thus reinforce the prayer's power and strength.

The extraordinary, evocative power of the prayer stick is best conveyed by this section of a Zuni prayer for the preparation of prayer sticks at the winter solstice:

> My children,
> All my children,
> Will make plume wands.
> My child,
> My father, sun,
> My mother, moon,
> All my children will clothe you with prayer plumes.
> When you have arrayed yourselves in these,
> With your waters,
> Your seeds
> You will bless all my children.
> All your good fortune

You will grant to them all.
To this end, my father,
My mother:
May I finish my road;
May I grow old;
May you bless me with life.

Prayer wheels. In the Tibetan tradition, as well as in the ancient cultures of the Egyptians, the Babylonians, and the Greeks, prayer wheels were the vehicles for setting prayer into motion or energizing it. The Tibetan prayer wheel, a cylinder with a small scroll within it, is set into rotation, symbolically connecting, through its circular motion, the person praying, the macrocosm, and the deities above. It releases the prayer by motion (just as, in other traditions, smoke transports prayer), while the rhythm of the spinning wheel permits the mind of the meditator to clear.

Rosary. The word *rosary* comes from the Latin for "rose garden," and it is the general term used both for the prayer beads of the Catholic, Hindu, Buddhist, and Muslim traditions and for the Catholic prayer. The Buddhist *mala* (the name in Sanskrit means "rose" or "garland") is composed of 108 beads and is used to count the number of mantras as an aid to meditation; a 27-bead *mala*, or funerary rosary, is used for meditations on impermanence and death. The Catholic rosary is used to focus on fifteen meditations on the life of Jesus and Mary, each punctuated by prayers and all counted out on the rosary beads. As a tool of meditation, it is meant, by its repetition, to free up the mind so that it focuses solely on the act of prayer.

Stupa. Originally a memorial monument to the historical Buddha or a reliquary of Buddhist saints, when placed on an altar, the stupa is a mandala of the enlightened mind of the Buddha.

Yantra. Like the mandala, the *yantra* is a graphic aid for meditation or, more accurately, the graphic equivalent of a mantra in Hinduism, composed of geometric signs round a center. The *yantra* is composed of upright triangles (with the apex at the top) representing Fire, Shiva, and the male principle and inverted triangles representing water, the womb, and the female principle, revolving around a center, or *bindu*. The Shri Yantra has four upright triangles and five inverted ones. The yantra also includes circles and lotus flowers, an external square with gateways at the four points of the compass, symbolizing the world, and Sanskrit letters.

Sounds and Energy

Sound, from the music or tone of instruments and from the human voice, is an integral part of ritual everywhere in the world. Many people invigorate both their sacred spaces and their domestic rituals with sound—whether with instruments or with their own voices raised in song, chant, or prayer or recordings. What we perceive as sound is really energy and vibration, the displacement or movement of molecules in the air, and all the space that surrounds us—indoors and out—is full of sound, whether or not we have the capacity to hear it. Just take a quiet moment in an empty room, and you will hear how filled with sound even "silence" is. Sound has the ability to relax and transform, both literally and figuratively; as Joseph Campbell has noted, rhythms—whether they are those of a Vedic chant or those of the shaman's drum—"are conceived of as wings, wings of spiritual transport."

The first sounds accompanying ritual were probably those of the human voice, clapping hands, and dancing feet, as shown by evidence from the Paleolithic; the sounds of the drum and the flute, too, may have echoed through the earliest sacred caves and caverns. The sistrum—a rattle made of a handle and frame fitted with loosely held rods—was sacred to the Egyptian goddesses Hathor and Bast and used in their ceremonies; later, it would become the sacral instrument of Isis, used in rites up through the time of the Roman Empire.

Many people use sound to clear their sacred places before they begin their rituals or prayers, to disperse energy or sound that could be counterproductive to ritual as well as to remove distracting sounds— the hum of a refrigerator, the noise of the street—that could impair spiritual openness. Oralee Stiles, a spiritual director who also helps other people build altars, uses a gong for group rituals because she feels its sound "allows people to shift more quickly from an outer space to an inner space" by getting rid of the "debris they came in with." For her, sound is a cleanser. To energize her altar, she may use sound or prayer or smudge.

Julie Middleton, the author of *Songs for Earthlings,* feels that each instrument used in ritual creates a different kind of energy: "Drums tap into the heartbeat of Earth and help organize our own scattered energies or rhythms so that they are more in synch with Earth. Rattles disperse energy or reorganize it. Wind chimes and Tibetan bowls calm our frantic, worldly energies and put us in a mood to listen or meditate."

Tom uses a silver bell, which he rings with certain chants; he feels that chanting focuses him and brings him "into the present," for chanting, he says, "lets you encompass the mundane and become larger than it." As a musician, he also well understands that "sound is very powerful: it bypasses your brain and goes straight to your heart." Julie Middleton adds, "When we sing, we become the instruments. Music helps open our hearts, and the words to songs share the human experience so that we know we are not alone. Chants take us past boredom and into a realm of light trance, similar to meditation, so that we can connect to the Higher Power."

Words are, of course, sounds with meaning, and they too play a tremendous role in energizing the sacred place, whether we call the combination of words we create chants, prayers, or invocations. Among the Navajo, words are so powerful that they provide the energy for things to happen; prayers are less like supplications than tools for invoking the divine. So powerful is the word that even the symbolic prayer—the prayer stick—can invoke a deity's presence. Many people follow Native American traditions by beginning with prayers or thanks to the four directions as they approach their altars.

The ability of words to express thoughts and feelings, to soothe and transform, and to connect us to one another as well as to the forces of the cosmos makes them perhaps the most potent form of energy and spirit at our disposal. The idea that words and prayer link the person praying to the deities, the individual voice to the greater voice that articulates all, is common to all forms of spirituality. The word is the ultimate tool of creation.

For anthologies of prayers, please see Resources, page 205–206.

Bells. In many cultures, the ringing of bells provided protection against evil spirits. Bell ringing was both cleansing and curative, and so in times of plague the steeple bells rang continuously. Their ringing, too, was thought to ward off the worst of storms. Emblems of potent magic and a higher power, they were used both to protect and to summon or placate a deity. The Feast of Osiris in ancient Egypt was ushered in by the ringing of bells; so, too, the church bells that ring all over Europe both call the faithful to worship and protect them on their way. The bells that are placed at the entrances of Shinto temples can be rung by petitioners so that their wishes may be granted.

In Buddhism, the handbell *(drilbu)*, symbolizing the feminine principle of wisdom as well as the world of the senses, is used in conjunction with the *dorje. See Dorjes.*

Chants. The monophonic sounds of chants are used for delivery of sacred texts or ritual formulae the world over; among the many examples are from the recitation of the Vedas, the incantations of shamans, or the ritual prayers and invocations of the Native Americans. Any word used repetitively will work as a chant or a mantra; the transformative power is in the rhythm and repetition.

Cymbals. The metallic sound of the cymbals punctuates quiet, and clashing cup- and bell-shaped cymbals were used to induce religious ecstasy in the Greek cults of Cybele and Dionysus and in the Roman rites of Attis. When used to make softer, tinkling sounds, cymbals have also been used in many cultures—by the ancient Hebrews and the Chinese, for example—to accompany rites.

Dorjes. Along with the *drilbu,* or handbell, the *dorje* is an important ritual instrument in Tantric Buddhism. Originally, the thunderbolt *(vajra)* or diamond clarity of the Hindu god Indra, the *dorje* represents the masculine path to enlightenment; *drilbu* and *dorje* together represent all reality contained within the enlightened Buddha.

Drums. The most sacred of all ritual instruments, the drum dates from the Neolithic and has religious and spiritual application the world over. Drums are associated with the earth and its gifts, as well as with the feminine: in Japan and China, barrel drums were filled with rice or rice hulls, while those of the Native American Ojibwa and Cree were filled with grain. What underlies its feminine and earth-bound symbolism is surely that the first sound we hear in the womb is the drumbeat of our mother's heart, and so the Egyptian god Bes, attendant at childbirth, is often pictured holding a drum.

Underscoring the drum's sacrality is that it is considered to be alive with spirit in many cultures, so much so that its creation was accompanied by rite and ceremony. According to Gladys Reichard, because the drum had the power to gather evil spirits among the Navajo, it was not a permanent fixture but rather a basket or a pot covered with skin that would be disposed of at the end of a ceremony. Shiva, the Hindu god of nature, the arts, dance, and learning, carries an hourglass-shaped drum that stands for sound, revelation, communication, and magic.

Drumming is a key element in shamanic practices and what Michael Harner has called "the shamanic state of consciousness." Harner relates how Siberian and other shamans call their drums "'the horse' or 'canoe' that transports them into the Lowerworld of Upperworld."

Flutes. One of the oldest of ceremonial instruments—examples carved out of bone with a single tone survive from the Paleolithic—the flute was associated with rebirth and thus has been found among grave goods in many cultures. It was sacred to the Babylonian god Dumuzi, or Tammuz, husband of Ishtar; when he played on his flute of lapis lazuli, the dead rose up. In Greek myth, Athena is credited with the invention of the flute. Among the Pueblo Indians, the flute was used to consecrate sacred objects and to communicate with the spirit world; it also played an important part in rain-making ceremonies. Kokopelli, trickster and spirit guide of the Pueblos, plays the flute.

Gongs. The chief musical instrument of Asia, the gong is endowed with many magical properties: the wind comes to its call, and it can drive out demons and grant wishes. It is also used ritually to begin and end periods of meditation.

Rattles. The sound of a rattle is usually considered an earth sound because it is released by natural elements; the world over, rattles are made from dried gourds and hooves, turtle shells, or other hollow objects filled with nuts, pebbles, beans, or crystals as well as in the form of anklets of shells. Rattle sounds can be used for cleansing space (they are used both in purification and exorcism ceremonies in many places), for mimetic magic (bringing forth rain or grain), or, because of their soft, percussive tones, for altering the individual's state of consciousness. Their sound can be soothing and relaxing; used rhythmically in conjunction with a drum, they are a key instrument in shamanic practices.

Tones. Essentially the intonation of single notes, toning is used by some people to energize or clear their sacred space or to relax themselves, getting their bodies loose and their breathing even. You don't need to be able to sing in order to tone.

Wind chimes. Wind chimes are, according to *feng shui* expert William Spear, used "to moderate or change *chi* flow." If the room in which you place your altar has some air flow, the sound of a wind chime will help focus your mind as well as relax you.

I built this motherhood altar to celebrate and honor my daughter's birthday and my first decade of motherhood. A beautiful reproduction of a twelfth-century Madonna and child looks down upon the altar, which has a babyhood picture of my child nestled amid candles, small vases full of flowers, and other objects. The small Mexican terra-cotta figure of birds at a feeder is on the altar to symbolize nature and nurturance, while the snakes and the shells are emblems of feminine energy and water. The goddess blessing bowl, created by Nancy Blair, holds a striated rock for earth and a heart for love, echoing the polished rock with a heart shape in the foreground. The delicate cowrie with its underside exposed celebrates the mystery of birth, while the contemporary Shona sculpture of a woman, from Zimbabwe, is a reminder of the beauty of the feminine.

Gemstones, Minerals, and Metals

In addition to conveying the owner's wealth or social status, gems, minerals, and metals have a long historical connection to the world of the spirit, and to altars in particular. Gems and minerals may be chosen for your altar on the basis of their beauty and shape, their color, their symbolic associations, their connections to systems such as *feng shui*, or their reputation as instruments of healing, magic, and energy. Perhaps what is most compelling about gems, minerals, and metals is their provenance: they are of the earth, and they remind us, whether they are polished or rough, of nature's enormous capacity for creating beauty.

It is no wonder, then, that so many gems and minerals have been associated, from ancient times, with the divine and the supernatural as well as the spiritual. The beauty and sparkle of the stones made ancient people ascribe supernatural origins to them, for they seemed like drops of divine essence left in the earth. Their ability to catch and sometimes refract the light into myriad rainbows made them a symbol of divine presence revealed, like the goddess Maya, whose rainbow, the bridge between earth and heaven, was often pictured as a necklace of gemstones. When highly polished, a stone or piece of metal became a mirror, mystically reflecting the hidden world of the spirit or soul. Carved with an image of the divine, as the Greek *baeytl* was, a gemstone became a sacred stone containing the deity within it. Pulverized or ground minerals served as pigments, sometimes with ritual purposes. Derived from hematite, red ocher is one of humanity's oldest ritual symbols; the dead were buried, covered, and stained with red ocher as early as 30,000 years ago in the caves of the Dordogne in France. Red, the color of blood, was thought to regenerate the dead, and, up through the first millennium, red ocher continued to stain images with the symbolic feminine life force. Gemstones and minerals have a history almost as old as amulets for warding off evil and bad fortune, as well as encouraging positive events: sacred eyes, scarabs, and other amulets carved out of or incised into gemstones and minerals protected the living and the dead the world over.

Because humans valued gemstones and metals for their beauty and rarity, they assumed that their deities would prize them equally; they were therefore among the earliest offerings placed on altars the world over. The mound builders of the Mississippi burned pearls as offerings, while burned gold and emerald were offered to the gods of the sun and the moon in New Granada. In the Hindu Rig Veda, it is written that "by giving gold the giver receives a life of light and glory," and elsewhere, specific gems and minerals are associated with specific benefits: coral subdues all three worlds; worshiping Krishna with rubies assures rebirth as a powerful emperor; a diamond will secure Nirvana; an emerald, the knowledge of the eternal. So, too, precious gems were left as offerings to the Virgin Mary by kings and queens in gratitude for her intercession.

Placed on your altar, a gemstone or mineral can become an object of meditation or the basis for a ritual. A clear piece of quartz with light shining upon it becomes the starting point for a meditation on the multiplicity of life, just as a blue stone—a piece of lapis lazuli or aquamarine—may recall the calm and depth of the oceans and waters. A piece of amber may provide a beginning for a reflection on the age of the earth and the cycles of life and change all things upon it experience. A lunar ritual can be made more meaningful by the addition of stones or metals associated with the moon; to invoke a feminine presence, use a gemstone or metal associated with her, such as copper for Aphrodite or carnelian for Isis.

Among the gemstones, minerals, and metals you may want to consider adding to your altar are those listed here; to use them for their color symbolism, please see page 44 and following.

Agate. A variegated quartz that comes in many colors, agate was once considered to be a tool of powerful magic, thought to turn an enemy's sword against its bearer and to cure the bites of snakes and the stings of scorpions. The Romans believed that an agate ring would appease the vegetative deities and yield a bountiful harvest. Agate is associated with the moon and the planet Mercury and dedicated to the month of June; it symbolizes health and longevity.

Amber. Not a mineral or gem, but the fossilized form of tree sap, yellow or golden brown in color, amber has long been prized as an amulet protecting against demons and the supernatural. The Greeks called it *elektron* (from which we derive the word *electricity*) for the way it attracts lightweight objects after it has been rubbed. In China, amber, or *hu po* (tiger's soul), was thought to be the transformed soul of the tiger left in the earth; it signified courage and imparted strong protective magic. In Greek as well as Scandinavian legend, amber was associated with the sorrow of the gods: for the Greeks, amber formed out of the tears shed by Meleager's sisters at his death, and when the Norse Odin wandered, Freya's falling tears became amber in the seas and gold in the earth.

Amethyst. Its name comes from the Greek, *amethystos* or "nonintoxicating," for the amethyst was long thought to prevent drunkenness. A mystical and beautiful stone, it was thought to control passion and keep evil thoughts in check as well as to quicken the intellect, as a Greek legend about its origins, recounted by George Fredrick Kunz, makes clear. Bacchus, the god of the grape, was angry and, in his pique, decided that the very first person he and his retinue encountered would be set upon by tigers. The hapless victim was a maiden named Amethyst who was on her way to worship at Diana's shrine. As the tigers approached, she appealed to the goddess, who turned her into shimmering quartz. Touched by the miracle and repentant, Bacchus poured the juice of the vine over the crystal as a libation, staining it purple as it remains to this day. In Lucan's account of the Isle of the Blessed, a city of gold with walls of emerald and temples of beryl, huge single amethysts were the altars. Amethyst was also known as the stone of atonement.

Aquamarine. A blue-green form of beryl, aquamarine means "seawater," and this stone is thought to protect sailors and ships.

Bloodstone. In Christian legend, bloodstone, green chalcedony marked with red, got its coloration when it was stained with Christ's blood as he hung on the cross. Like other red stones, such as the ruby and garnet, bloodstone was thought to be effective against inflammation and hemorrhage; it was also a source of calm and a potential cure for discord. Barbara Walker, in *The Book of Sacred Stones*, recommends using bloodstone as a meditative stone because its coloration suggests the "correlations between the red lifeblood of animals and the nurturing powers of the green plant world."

Carnelian. In ancient Egypt, carnelian, transparent red chalcedony, was known as the "blood of Isis" and was placed on the necks of the dead or set into rings to aid in the process of resurrection. Muhammad wore a carnelian ring, and, among Muslims, it is thought to preserve tranquillity in the midst of troubles and to keep the wearer blessed and happy. Carnelian has a reputation for driving away evil spirits and bad dreams, as well as counteracting the effects of sorcery.

Copper. In many cultures, copper was both a useful metal, suitable for tools and weaponry, and a sacred one. It is associated with both gods, such as the fire god of Babylonia, and goddesses, including Astarte and Aphrodite (Venus). In Latin, copper was known as the "metal from Cyprus" (*aes cuprum*), the island sacred to Aphrodite, who was born in the surrounding seas. The magic mirror of Venus used for divination was thought to be made of polished copper, which may have encouraged its association with powers of healing. In Native American traditions, copper was a sacred metal used for sacrificial instruments as well as ornaments; the tribes around Lake Superior identified lumps of copper as divinities or the gifts of the water gods.

Coral. The "tree of the sea," coral symbolizes the world of the waters and has the ancient reputation of warding off the forces of evil, probably because, as recorded in Ovid's *Metamorphoses,* red coral was believed to have been formed by the drops of blood that fell into the seas from Medusa's head. In China, coral is associated with longevity; in Navajo sandpainting, the rain gods are depicted wearing necklaces of coral. Today, as the coral reefs of the ocean suffer deterioration from waste and toxins, a piece of coral may symbolize the fragility of the ecosystem and of life in general.

Diamond. As the hardest of all gems and one of the rarest and most costly, diamond is rightly named World Goddess; because of their hardness, diamonds were thought to have dominion over other stones and were therefore considered to be sacred to the Mother of the Gods. Long associated with the sun, light, life, and purity, the diamond has many spiritual connotations, including one connected to the Virgin Mary.

In Buddhism, the seat of enlightenment is known as the "diamond throne," for it was told that once a wondrous throne carved out of a single diamond, one hundred feet in circumference, had stood near the Tree of Knowledge, where the supreme truth, known as the "ecstasy of the diamond," was revealed to Buddha. The throne itself was immutable, the only thing on the earth impervious to earthquakes, storms, and the forces of nature. Time, though, has covered the diamond throne with sand and earth. Elsewhere, the diamond is associated with moral and intellectual knowledge.

Emerald. One of the rarest and most costly of stones, the emerald has a history as a revealer of truth and is regarded as having the ability to help divine the future; it was thought, too, to strengthen the memory and the eloquence of its wearer. The emerald was sacred to Venus, its green hue symbolic of the reproductive force. In rabbinical legend, there were four precious stones that endowed the wise Solomon with the power over all creation; the emerald was one of them. At the time of the Spanish conquest, an emerald goddess—an extraordinary stone—was worshiped by the ancient Peruvians as the goddess Umiña; it was only shown to the faithful on feast days, when offerings of "daughters"—other emeralds—were given to her. In India, an emerald was the most precious of offerings because it assured eternal life. As amulets, emeralds were thought to be extremely powerful, assuring safety on the seas, good fortune, protection against spirits and dragons, as well as health.

Garnet. A red stone, the garnet has a long association with blood as well as with the feminine. Its name comes from *granatum,* or pomegranate, a fruit that for millennia stood for the womb and its multifold gifts. It is an appropriate stone for earth or other feminine rituals.

Gold. The embodiment of solar light and divine intelligence, gold has long been perceived as the most precious of metals; as far back as the Neolithic, religious and spiritual artifacts have been made of gold. Because it does not tarnish and seems impervious to the ravages of time, gold was also associated with immortality; the Egyptians fashioned caskets out of gold so as to confer eternal life on the remains they contained. Gold was also considered the purest of metals and therefore thought to preserve the innate strengths and powers of sacred or medicinal herbs. Just as the Druids were said to have harvested their sacred mistletoe with sickles of gold, so, too, medieval herbalists used golden implements. In China, gold, or *chin,* is considered solar and yang in nature; silver, the metal of the moon, is yin.

Hematite. Its name means "bloodstone," a reflection of the bloodlike liquid produced when ground hematite is mixed with water. Although it may be silvery, red-brown, or black on the exterior, hematite is always distinguished by its bloodlike streaks. Because hematite yields red ocher, the sacred symbolic blood of ancient times, it is associated with rebirth as well as protection; it was considered sacred to the god of war, Mars.

Jade. An extremely important stone for the cultures of China and ancient Mexico, two separate gemstones are known as jade: jadeite and nephrite. In China, jade is associated with immortality as well as with yang, the vital masculine principle, and so, as an amulet, it was buried with the dead to revitalize their spirits. Jade also symbolized the five cardinal virtues: charity, modesty, justice, courage, and wisdom. In Taoism, the supreme heavenly god is known as "the jade emperor," or *Yu Ti*. In Olmec tradition, jade was used for sacred carvings and was placed in the sarcophagi of the dead. The water goddess of the Olmecs, Chalchihuitlicue, was known as "She of the Jade Loincloth."

Lapis lazuli. Long associated with water because of its brilliant blue color, lapis lazuli was in ancient Egypt the favored stone for carved figures of the goddesses, especially Maat, goddess of truth, who weighed the souls of the dead against her feather. The Egyptians also placed lapis lazuli within the embalmed bodies of the dead in place of the heart. In Sumer, lapis lazuli was associated with resurrection: the flute of Dumuzi, or Tammuz, the sound of which brought the dead back to life, was made of lapis. In China, lapis lazuli ornamented the girdles of the Manchu emperors as they worshiped at the Temple of Heaven. In the Christian tradition, lapis lazuli is the emblem of chastity and ensures help from angels.

Lead. An element with dark associations, lead was sacred to Saturn, god of the underworld for the Romans, and was considered to have magical powers; it was used for divination, as well as for casting both spells and curses (by writing them on a lead tablet) or, equally, as protection against spells (by wearing a thin plate of lead over the chest).

Malachite. Because it is found near copper deposits and because it is also green, malachite is closely associated with the metal sacred to the goddess Aphrodite. Both the Greeks and the Romans identified it as a stone possessed of great magical powers; the Romans considered it sacred to Juno and called it the "peacock stone" in honor of Juno's sacred bird. Cut into a triangle—the shape symbolizing the feminine—malachite was effective against evil.

Obsidian. The volcanic glass known as obsidian has long been highly prized, both for its ceremonial and ritualistic uses and for the manufacture of spears, arrowheads, and knives. In the Americas, obsidian was important to many tribes; bear shamans wore shards of obsidian on their sleeves to imitate the bear's slashing claws; while the Wailaki and Yuki of California used obsidian for ceremonial objects in initiation rites. In Mexico, obsidian was used for statues of the god Tezcatlipoca, or "the shining god"; mirrors used for divination were made of polished obsidian.

Opal. Its name comes from the Sanskrit for "valuable stone," and opal was prized in antiquity, as now, for its fiery iridescence. The Romans associated it with prophecy and foresight.

Pearl. For thousands of years, the circular shape of a pearl identified it with perfection, while its shimmer associated it with the moon and, by extension, the feminine. In ancient Greece, it was associated with Aphrodite, who was born out of the foam of the sea. A pearl is neither gemstone nor mineral, of course, but the product of a bivalve, and, as the treasure hidden within the shell, for the Gnostics and others, it signified hidden knowledge. In Christian symbolism, Mary was the oyster, and Christ was the pearl. In China, the pearl was one of the "eight jewels" and symbolized the pure and the precious.

Quartz. Clear quartz is also known as "rock crystal," associated in many cultures with divination, whence the "crystal ball" of gypsies and charlatans alike. The Roman priestesses of Vesta kindled the sacred altar fires with quartz, drawing fire down from the heavens; to permit the fires to go out was to face certain death. The Greeks called quartz *krystallos,* or "ice," in the belief that it was ice that had been permanently frozen; the Japanese knew it as the congealed breath of the White Dragon. Because the dragon was an emblem of the highest powers of creation, rock crystal was the perfect jewel, symbol of infinity and space, perfection, patience, and perseverance.

Used as a divining stone by the Cherokees, and on the tops of ceremonial wands by other Native American shamans, quartz was cleansed with deer blood and kept in special ceremonial pouches. Because the "clear stone" was thought to induce visions, the Apaches used it to locate lost property, especially horses. Among the Navajo, rock crystal is a ceremonial stone, often used symbolically to represent fire. Even more important, according to Gladys A. Reichard's *Navaho Religion,* at the moment of creation, a crystal was placed in the mouth of each person so that everything said would come true. Thus, each Navajo pollen bag had a crystal within to empower the prayers of its carrier.

Ruby. Its red color associated the ruby with both the planet Mars and the sun; it was thought a potent talisman against perils, as well as an antidote to bad dreams and depression. When the gem was dropped into water, the "fire" within it was reputed to bring water to a boil. In Sanskrit, it was known as the "king of precious stones" *(ratnaraj);* its color was sacred, as "red as the lotus" *(padmarâga).* The Muslim angel who bears the world on his shoulders stands on a ruby rock. In Hindu tradition, the owner of a ruby could live amid his enemies in safety and would be protected from storms.

Sapphire. The blue color of a sapphire made it a gem of the heavens, associated with air as well as with Venus and Saturn; thought to be a prophetic stone, it was reputed to influence spirits and, thus, was thought to be a favorite of witches. In Hindi, the sapphire is called "the beloved of Saturn" (*saniprijam*) or "sacred to Saturn" (*saurinata*). Tradition held that the Ten Commandments were inscribed on a tablet of sapphire, although this was probably a confusion of sapphire and lapis lazuli.

Silver. A powerful metal associated with moon goddesses in many cultures, silver was also thought, at certain of the lunar phases, to induce oracular dreams in the wearer; its alchemical symbol was a crescent moon, and it was associated with birth. Widely used the world over for sacred ceremonies, it was particularly valued for bells and musical instruments and as an effective repellent of evil spirits. For the Muslims, the second heaven was that of silver, and so prayers and charms are mounted or written on silver to increase their effectiveness. The bones of the Egyptian god Ra were thought to be silver, his members gold, and his hair lapis lazuli.

Tigereye. The beautiful tigereye hints of hidden mysteries and secrets, the shifting light within it hidden one moment and revealed the next. Carved amulets of tigereye were thought to offer protection to Roman soldiers during battle. People I have spoken to use tigereye on their altars to symbolize the hidden treasures of the earth, but perhaps the most lyrical suggestion comes from Barbara Walker in *The Book of Sacred Stones:* "Polished tigereye is a wonderful symbol of cyclic reality, the alternation of light and dark in the world of nature and of time." It is thus a fitting stone for any altar dedicated to change and growth.

Tin. Sacred to Jupiter, tin was used for divination. Although it has the modern connotation of cheap or flimsy, tin was traditionally an important metal used in the making of bronze.

Tourmaline. A gemstone that was only discovered in the eighteenth century, tourmaline occurs in over one hundred colors and is thus more interesting for its hues than for its meaning or symbolism.

Turquoise. A sacred stone in many cultures the world over, turquoise is dedicated to Saturn and associated with December. In ancient Egypt, it was sacred to the cow-headed goddess Hathor; in Tibet, it protected against the evil eye. It is the most important holy stone of the Native American tribes of the southwestern United States, offering protection against evil spirits and, mixed with cornmeal, used as an offering to the gods. In the Native American pueblos, lumps of turquoise are buried in the ground as offerings to the gods when a house or a kiva is built. The Navajo regarded the turquoise as the heart of Mother Earth, while the Zuni told that the sky was blue because of the reflection of the sacred turquoise mountain. Among the Aztecs, turquoise, or *xihuitl,* was one of the most revered of the gemstones that decorated the shields and diadems of kings. Turquoise was also an important component of Aztec mythology: the god of fire, Xiuhtecutli, was called the Lord of the Turquoise, for the stone signified the unity of solar and earthly fire. Xuihcoat, the sacred serpent, was adorned with turquoise. The finest turquoise, *teuxivitl,* or "turquoise of the gods," unlined and unmarked, was not permitted to be owned or worn by humans; it was strictly used for rituals in service of the gods.

Animals, Totems, and Guardians

Long before the Book of Genesis assigned Adam dominion over the animals and thus established a Judeo-Christian hierarchy of man over beast, humanity perceived animals as manifestations of the divine spirit in creation. Animals were worshiped for their strength and power and as the dwelling places of divine spirit, for certain deities were believed to be incarnate in them. Over time, the animals themselves became epiphanies of the divine spirit.

From the period of the Paleolithic forward, when animal figures were painted and incised on the walls of sacred caves, to the Neolithic and beyond, when statuettes of the Mother Goddess showed her with the attributes of many of her epiphanies—the nurturing bear, the energizing snake, the owl of death, and the life-giving sow—animals and the sacred were inseparable. In ancient Egypt, the gods and goddesses took on animal form: Hathor the cow, Anubis the jackal, Bast the cat, Neith the cobra, among others. Not only were the gods and goddesses of ancient Greece honored by animal sacrifice, but their attributes were represented by animals who embodied them: Athena's wisdom by the owl, Artemis's protection by the bear, Hera's watchfulness by the peacock and the "eyes" in its feathers.

Other traditions, including Native American ones, assumed a spiritual relationship not only between humanity and animals in general, but among individuals, tribes, and families and individual animals specifically. Totems—the word means "his sibling kin" or simply "my kin" in Ojibwa and Algonquian—were the animals regarded as either the mythical ancestors of a clan or family or their guardian or protector. Each individual has at least one animal spirit guardian, although, according to Michael Harner in his *Way of the Shaman,* among certain tribes it was believed that a given individual could fail to connect with his guardian. Shamans depend on their spirit guides, or power animals, to accompany them into the world of the spirit. Among the Zuni, fetishes carved in the shape of animals were not only used for the supplication of hunters and for rites of thanksgiving for a successful hunt, but also as powerful spiritual tools for shamans and priests. The Native American medicine wheel, too, is associated with animal spirits or guardians.

Animal shapes and figures have long been used to adorn and impart sacred energy to altars and ritual places. A miniature bench-shaped altar from the fifth millennium Cucuteni civilization was excavated with sixteen snake-headed sculptures seated on chairs with horns. Next to the altar was a life-size chair, also decorated with horns, which may well have been the seat of the residing priestess; close by was a bread oven that had the remains of burned animal bones within it. A relief of a snake, emblematic of the Goddess's life-giving energy, adorns a pillar near a ritual hearth in the Ggantija temple in Malta, while a procession of carved animals in relief—a ram, a pig, and three goats—runs along the side of the altar of the Maltese Tarxien temple. Underground Sardinian tombs have sculpted bulls' heads and horns above their entrances and also within them; figures of lions guarded and protected ancient Egyptian tombs and Assyrian temples. In Minoan civilization, the Goddess's epiphany would be represented in many animal forms—in the snake, the horns of the bull, the butterfly and the bee, and the dove, among others—and sacred libations would be poured from a black soapstone rhyton shaped like a bull's head with gilded wooden horns and inlaid eyes of jasper and rock crystal. A fresco from Knossos on Crete depicts the ritual bull dance, a sacral celebration of nature and its powers. In ancient Greece, the protection offered to women in childbed by the virgin goddess Artemis would be celebrated every five years at Brauron, one of her chief sanctuaries, by women and girls dressed as bears, symbolic of the goddess's protection. Her priestesses were called "little bears."

Representations of animals can be used to empower your altar by acting as symbols of their strength and energy or as guardian spirits or totems. Many of the people I have met who have adopted and used animals as allies or totems have felt strong personal connections to the animal they identify with. Rick has been drawn to bears for their strength and dexterity since he was a young boy and encountered them in the wild in the Pacific Northwest. As an adult, he considers the bear a protector guardian. He never leaves the house without a symbol of the bear with him (he wears bear-print bracelets and a

Navajo bear stone fetish around his neck), and his altar has a wood-carved figure of a bear on it. Many of us who have lived in urban or suburban areas have little first-hand knowledge of animals other than domestic ones or a limited range of birds, squirrels, chipmunks, and raccoons, and draw our sense of connection to specific animals from reading as well as from films and documentaries. One woman I know has adopted the wolf as her special guardian for its incredible will to survive under the most trying of ecological circumstances. For her, the wolf is both an exemplar of survival in the modern world *and* a personal protector. Still others have encountered their animal totems in dreams.

Ultimately, the animal or animals you select to make a part of your altar can be chosen for any reason or, as my friend Ed has, for no conscious reason: his carved turquoise dolphin fetish is part of his altar simply because he was drawn to it. Sometimes, the animals we choose instinctively for our sacred spaces yield enlightening surprises. I chose to put reproductions of Egyptian blue faience hippos amid my Mother Goddesses simply because I found them beautiful; it was a magical moment when I later discovered that, for the Egyptians, the hippo was a guardian of pregnant women. On a much more conscious level, I surround my statues of goddesses with snakes, signifying feminine energy, while a giraffe and a zebra stand close to an African Ashanti goddess.

An entire altar can be devoted to animals, either wild or domestic. Linda, a psychotherapist, has in her office a small permanent altar devoted to the owl. Set on a dark blue cloth, small statues and pictures of owls are surrounded by clear crystals and egg-shaped stones, bringing what Linda sees as "the owl's ability to see to the heart of things, even in the dark" to the work she does with her patients. Nancy Blair has a cat altar in her living room; it is laden with images of feline familiars—statues of the Egyptian Bast, Sekhmet, and the Key Marco cat—set against an amethyst geode to bring energy into the room. Her own real-life cat, Max, whose photograph rests against the geode, was originally a rough-and-tumble tom with an urban background. He has taught Nancy many lessons about the wild and the tame, as well as nature, and she sees the altar as bringing that energy into her living space. She sometimes reconsecrates her cat altar by collecting Max's shed whiskers and tying them up with a golden string, rather like a sheaf of wheat. The altar is, as she says, "a prayer for Max and his spirit."

What follows is, of course, only a sampling of animals that can be used to empower and enrich your sacred space; for further reading, please see page 207.

Bear. In many cultures of the Northern Hemisphere, the bear was both an admired and a sacred animal. We can imagine that humanity from the beginning often came into contact with bears who shared the caves in which humans lived and worshiped. The sacral nature of the bear was perhaps celebrated over 75,000 years ago, for, in a cave high in the Swiss Alps, row upon row of arranged bear skulls were found, indicating both ritual sacrifice and worship of the bear. The bear's hibernation and then its reemergence in the spring with its cubs made it a potent symbol of rebirth and regeneration, closely tied to the earth and the Earth Mother, as is made clear from the Neolithic onward by statuettes and pots of the bear as the mother and nurse, often cradling a child in her arms.

Bee. Though in familiar homilies the bee is largely congratulated for its industry ("as busy as a bee"), the bee is an ancient symbol of the sacred feminine. In ancient Egypt, the bee was a symbol of royalty and, for its making of honey, of creativity and wealth. Bees were called the "tears of Ra," the sun god. Because bees were thought to come to life in bull's carcasses, the bee, like the butterfly, was a symbol of the Goddess's powers of regeneration. The intricacy of the honeycomb's cells and the sacred sweetness—honey—that exuded from them made the comb and the hive a symbol of the richness and connectiveness of all things within the Goddess. (See "Honey," page 143, for more.) Even the buzzing sound of the bee was an epiphany of the Goddess's presence; in his *Georgics,* Virgil describes the cymbals used to attract swarming bees as belonging to "the Great Mother." The priests and priestesses of the sacred rites at Demeter's precinct, Eleusis, were called *melissae* ("bees"), and Artemis was symbolized as the bee at Ephesus, site of the springtime festival.

Bird. Its wings, its flight, and its ability to move between the realms of earth and heaven made the bird a symbol of the spirit, or the soul, and its transcendence over the material world. In many cultures, birds were considered messengers from the spirit world who communicated the secrets of the gods and goddesses. Thus, among the Greeks and the Romans, the flight patterns of birds were signs of divine will and the primary source of augury. The bird was both magical and mysterious, and, from the earliest times, by putting on its feathers and wings, a shaman could reach the spirit world. In Latin a single word—*aves*—meant both "birds" and "spirits." In many cultures, including Native American ones, the bird's magic was so potent that even a single feather could put the wearer in touch with the world of the spirit.

Images of birds, as well as actual feathers, are important and valuable additions to the spiritual content of any altar. Marilyn Goldman puts feathers in her outdoor altar—a green, weathered niche hanging on a post in an arbor—as well as gifts of roses from her garden and small rocks to acknowledge the splendor of nature. For Julie Middleton, the presence of a feather on her altar is a reminder of air, new ideas, and starting over.

Bull. An extremely sacral animal, which once represented the feminine and became an emblem of the masculine, the bull is connected to both the moon and the sun.

Butterfly. In Minoan culture, the butterfly—often represented schematically as two interlocking triangles—was associated with the goddess of death and regeneration, as well as with the *labrys*, or double ax. In Greek, one word, *psyche*, means both "butterfly" and "soul," and, for both its extraordinary transformation from caterpillar to pupa to its rebirth as a butterfly and its attraction to the light, this beautiful insect has been an emblem of the soul, the spirit, and rebirth. Among the Aztecs, the butterfly was an attribute of Xochipilli, the god of vegetation. The Chinese associated the butterfly with joy and summer. In Christian symbolism, the butterfly's ancient connection to rebirth made it a symbol of Christ's resurrection. In Native American traditions, the butterfly has both positive and negative attributes. Among the Hopi, the Butterfly Kachina, Palhikwmana, is an emblem of fertility; in contrast, among the Zuni, the sacred butterfly, Lahacoma, is but a lure for unsuspecting humans about to be tricked by dangerous kachinas.

What we know about butterflies—the three-thousand-mile migration of the monarch, for example—only increases our admiration for them. A fitting guardian and emblem of spiritual transformation, the butterfly can give your sacred space the lightness of being it needs.

Cat. The cat goddess of ancient Egypt, Bast, was a deity of fire, closely associated with the heat and light of the sun and the sun god Ra, as well as the growth of all vegetation and the ripening of the seed. At the same time, she was also a lunar deity, presiding over pregnant women and childbed. Cats were sacral animals in Egypt, buried with great veneration and luxury. In Greece and Rome, cats were also associated with the lunar goddesses, Artemis and Diana; the Norse goddess Freya drove in a chariot drawn by cats. Grain goddesses, closely connected to fecundity and motherhood, were often pictured as cats, the Greek Demeter and the Celtic Cerridwen among them, an association that would finally culminate in the Christian legend of the *Gatto della Madonna,* or "Our Lady's cat." The story recounts how, at precisely the same time as the Virgin Mary gave birth to the infant Jesus, a cat under the floorboards of the humble stable gave birth to a litter of kittens.

The black cat, though, was long thought to have magical powers, probably because of its association with the goddesses of the underworld, the Greek Hecate and the Germanic Hel. It was but a small patriarchal leap from these associations to those of the witch and her evil familiar.

Cow. One of the most important symbolic sacred animals, the cow is firmly connected to the fruition of the earth as well as the moon, and to motherhood and birth, as well as to the primal food, milk. (See page 144.) In ancient Egypt, the cow-faced Hathor was a cosmic goddess, queen of the heavens and called Mother of Light, the birth of which was the first creation. She takes on the cow head as a goddess of both birth and death: she is the Lady of the Southern Sycamore, an emblem of birth, and the Lady of the Holy Land, or underworld, as which she is sometimes represented as a cow walking away from the funereal mountain. The goddess Nut also took on the shape of a cow; her belly was covered in stars, representing the heavens. In Norse myth, the cow Andumla created the first man by licking him out of a block of salty ice.

Crane. Because of its ability to fly long distances seemingly without effort, the crane was an emblem of strength; its wings were used as amulets against fatigue. Because the crane migrated, its return signaled the coming of spring; thus the crane became a symbol of rebirth. In ancient Greece, the crane was sacred to Demeter. In China, the crane is a symbol of wisdom and longevity; it is also thought to transport to heaven souls who have attained immortality.

Crow. Although in European symbolism the carrion-eating crow is not always distinguishable from the raven and often has negative associations, on the North American continent, the crow is often a creator of the world (as among the Tlingit) or a trickster figure.

Sheltered by the energy-releasing beauty of a large amethyst geode, sculptor Nancy Blair's own statues of feline goddesses make this altar a different kind of spiritual haven. From left to right, the Egyptian Bast, goddess of music and dance; a vision of the maternal Bast, her kittens at her feet; the lion-headed Sekhmet, Egyptian goddess of the sun and protector of the weak; and the Key Marcos Panther, found sunken in Florida's waters, surround a photograph of her cat on this special altar dedicated to the feline.

Deer. Incredibly fleet of foot, the deer was associated, from ancient times, with energy, fecundity, and the moon, for just as the moon grew, died, and was reborn in the night sky, so the deer could grow, shed, and then regrow its mighty antlers. Shamans the world over, from France to Siberia to China, put on the antlers of the deer to take on the animal's magical powers. In ancient Greece, the deer was sacred to Artemis, goddess of the untamed wilderness, to whom the bear and lion were also sacred.

Dog. An animal possessed of great loyalty as well as protectiveness, the dog was a divinity of the moon goddess as early as the Neolithic, associated with death and night. On Neolithic seals and pots, dogs guard the Tree of Life. Cerberus, the three-headed dog, guarded the entrance to the underworld in Greek myth, while wild dogs accompanied the crone goddess of the moon, Hecate. In ancient Egypt, the god Anubis, protector of the dead, was portrayed with the head of either a wild dog or a jackal. Anubis, whose name means "time," prepared the mummy for the journey into the afterlife. He was also the guardian of the dividing point between the visible and invisible worlds, between life and death, watchful, as all dogs are, in both light and darkness, day and night. The annual flooding of the Nile—the moment at which the rich silt from the highlands enriched the soil—took place each year after the brightest star in the sky, Sirius, or the Dog Star, rose at daybreak, very close to September 10. In Celtic mythology, a dog was the companion of Epona, goddess of the hunt. In ancient Mexico, dogs were buried with the dead to serve as guides to the underworld.

Dolphin. A fresco of dolphins adorns the sacred precinct of Knossos on Crete; the Greek Aphrodite, goddess of the sea and love, born out of the waves, rides on the backs of dolphins. While to modern eyes these friendly mammals (as we now know them to be) have become symbols of animal intelligence as well as the victims of human uncaring, the dolphin has a rich and ancient mythological history. Apollo took the form of a dolphin to found his temple at Delphi; Dionysus, who was also worshiped at Delphi, is associated with the dolphin as well. Much earlier, in sculptures from the East, the dolphin was an attribute of Atgargatis, mother goddess of vegetation, nourisher of life, and receiver of the dead who would be born again. The connection between the dolphin and rebirth occurs as well in Etruscan myth: the souls of dead were carried by dolphins to the Islands of the Blessed. Dolphins were thought to have once been human, and so they were credited with both miraculous rescues of sailors at sea and of children who were unlucky enough to be pulled under by the great waters.

On a contemporary altar, the image of the dolphin signifies the interconnectedness of all forms of life and the great beauty that resides in the planet's deep waters.

Dove. Although over time the dove has become primarily a symbol of peace, it was an important part of rite and ritual in ancient times, associated with augury and divination. The dove was an epiphany of the Goddess in Minoan civilization, and was sacred to Astarte, Inanna, Isis, Aphrodite, and later Venus, who was known on Cyprus as the Lady of Trees and Doves. The priestesses at the sacred grove of Dodona, ancient Greece's oldest oracular center, were called *peleiae,* or "doves." Zeus and Dione were worshiped at Dodona, said to have been established when a black dove from Egyptian Thebes settled on the branches of an ancient oak. The priestesses at Dodona prophesied beneath the branches of the holy oak and interpreted the cooing of the doves, the rustling of their wings, and the clanging of chimes hung in the oak's branches. In India, the dove was a symbol of the soul. The dove is an important symbol in the Judeo-Christian tradition as well; it is a dove who appears to Noah after the flood, and, at the moment of Christ's baptism, the Holy Spirit descends in the form of a dove.

Dragon. Although the dragon is a malevolent being in the West, in the Orient it is the ultimate symbol and embodiment of the spirit of transformation and change and thus a potent emblem of the life force. Chief among the aquatic animals (as the tiger was among the land animals), the dragon was thought to emerge every spring, the essence of the productive force of water and moisture; every autumn, it would descend into the waters, covering itself in mud by the autumnal equinox, waiting to reemerge the following spring. It signifies strength and goodness and was the essence of *yang,* the male element, as the tiger symbolizes *yin.* The turquoise dragon, symbol of the spring rain and the East, was the fifth sign of the zodiac; the white dragon, the emblem of death and the West. In Japan, the dragon is the embodiment of the life-giving waters. At the opposite end of the spectrum, in Western traditions, the dragon is associated with fire, chaos, and bestiality and, in Christianity, with the diabolical.

Eagle. The eagle is the most regal of all birds; its keen vision, its ability to soar to great heights, its longevity, and the extraordinary inaccessibility of its nests have made it a creature of tremendous spiritual import. In Greek myth, the oracular center of Greece, Delphi, and the *omphalos,* or "navel" of the world, was established when Zeus let fly two eagles from the opposite extremes of the world. Sacred to Zeus, the eagle was thought to be impervious to lightning and thunder; thus eagle wings became powerful amulets, sometimes buried in the fields against those natural forces. In the Rig Veda, an eagle brings the sacred soma to humanity. A special mythology grew up around the eagle that emphasized its powers of renewal and regeneration: it was thought that, alone among the creatures, the eagle stayed young and renewed its plumage by flying close to the sun and then diving into the depths of the waters. This imagery appears in the Old Testament; in the New Testament, the eagle is a symbol of Christ's resurrection and is associated with Saint John as an emblem of the spiritual heights he achieved. Reputed to slay both snakes and dragons, the eagle was also a symbol of the triumph of good over evil and of spiritual contemplation.

Among the Aztecs, Cihaucoatl, or "Snake Woman," was also known as "Eagle Woman" (Quauh-Cihuatl) for her crown of eagle feathers; she symbolized all women who had died in childbirth. In our contemporary times, the eagle also symbolizes the fragility of our ecosystems. For the Native Americans, the eagle was a bird of power whose feathers were of ritual and symbolic importance, as they continue to be to this day.

Elephant. Everything we have come to learn about the emotional complexity of elephants only increases our admiration for these magnificent, endangered animals. Not surprisingly, elephants have, in many cultures, extremely positive associations. Throughout Asia, the elephant is honored for its intelligence; in Hinduism, Ganesha, the god of writing and wisdom, has the head of an elephant. The birth of Buddha was announced by a white elephant, and the elephant is a symbol of the one who brings salvation from worldly chaos. The elephant is also associated with the Hindu goddess Lakshmi, bestower of health, wealth, as well as offspring; the white elephant of rain and fertility is particularly important to her.

Fish. The fruit of the earth's waters, the fish has long been associated with divinity; in humanity's early history, it was firmly associated with the divine feminine and birth, as artifacts from the Paleolithic and Neolithic make clear. Artemis, goddess of wilderness and childbirth, is associated with the fish. In the Orient, the fish is an auspicious symbol, signifying happiness; in a creation myth, the islands of Japan were said to have been created by the thrashing of a giant carp who started a tidal wave out of which the islands rose. The fish stands for strength and endurance. In Christian symbolism, the fish is an emblem of Christ, derived from the Greek for fish, *ichthys,* the five letters of which were understood as standing for "Jesus Christ God's Son Savior."

Frog. The frog has been associated with regeneration and change since ancient times, doubtless because of its extraordinary metamorphosis from egg to tadpole to four-legged creature. Not surprisingly, it is also associated with magic. From the Neolithic onward, carved frogs—made of various stones and minerals—as well as engraved representations on vases and other artifacts appear with vulvae or triangles, testifying to the link between the frog and birth. The frog was sacred to Hekat, or Hequet, goddess of the midwives in ancient Egypt; Hekat was also credited, along with a frog god, with the creation of the world. For the Aztecs, the frog was an epiphany of the goddess Chalchihuitlicue, the lady of the green jade skirts and the underworld deity of the flowing waters.

I use images of frogs on my altar and elsewhere to symbolize transformation.

Goose. Associated with the wind, perhaps because of its sibilant hiss, the goose was sacred to Aphrodite, who was pictured as Goddess of Heaven in a chariot drawn by swans and geese, and the Roman Juno, as Queen of Heaven. Brahma, as the Breath of Life, is often pictured riding on a goose.

Hippopotamus. The Greeks gave it the name by which we know it, *hippopotamus,* literally "river horse," even though, because hippos were not indigenous to Greece, they were sketchy about what the animal looked like. In ancient Egypt, even though the hippo was sometimes seen as a "slayer of Osiris" because of its habit of ravaging the crops, its rotund belly made it a deity as well. Tauret, the Great One—also known as Rert or Sheput—was depicted as a hippo on its hind legs with a woman's breasts. A beneficent spirit, she was a protector of women in childbirth, and amulets depicting Tauret were often placed on the abdomens of women in childbed. The hippo then is a fitting guardian for an altar or ritual involving birth and motherhood.

Horse. From the Paleolithic, when equine forms were drawn on the walls of the sacred caves, to the present, the horse has been a powerful and admirable animal with close connections to gods and goddesses as well as to humans. Demeter was sometimes portrayed with a horse's head, while Poseidon, Athena, and Aphrodite all had horse aspects. The horse was associated with thunder, thought to be the sound of its hooves, as well as the gods who rode chariots, the Greek sun god Helios, the Hindu god of the sun Surya, and the Norse Thor among them. Though the horse is often perceived as masculine, the deity of the horse was Epona, a goddess of fertility as well as the inventor of language, who was worshiped by the Romans even though she was probably of Gallic origin. Romans placed an image of the goddess, sometimes crowned with flowers, in a shrine near the center of the stable. The horse is also a symbol of wisdom, sometimes associated with clairvoyance.

Lion. Although it has, over time, become connected to the sun, royalty, and masculinity, the lion as well as the lioness were the counterparts to the goddesses Cybele, Artemis, and the Roman Fortuna, who were often depicted riding on or accompanied by lions. At the eighth-millennium city of Çatal Hüyük, a birth-giving Goddess was shown flanked by lions or leopards, an early representation of the lion as symbolic of the maternal. Lions were protector spirits, too, who guarded the entrances to Egyptian tombs and Assyrian temples. While the Egyptian sun god Ra took the form of a lion, the goddess Sekhmet and sometimes the goddess Bast were depicted with the heads of lionesses, personifying the scorching rays of the sun. In Buddhism, the lion is a symbol of constancy, courage, and nobility and a harbinger of good luck.

Owl. Its large eyes and its remarkably acute vision gave the owl a reputation for seeing to the heart of things; in addition to being the epiphany of the goddess Athena's wisdom, the owl was credited with both oracular powers and protection against evil spirits. At the same time, this nocturnal creature has, since Neolithic times (and perhaps even before), been associated with darkness, night, and death; in Egypt, the owl was the hieroglyph for death. Snowy owls are engraved on a wall of the Upper Paleolithic cave of Les Trois Frères in France. Even when the round eyes of the owl signified the death aspect of the feminine life force, as they did on pots, vases, and steles from the Neolithic forward, they were balanced, as Marija Gimbutas has shown, by zigzags, spirals, and labyrinthine designs that signified the life force and regeneration. The owl, then, is a comforter of the bereaved as well; in Mycenean Greece, tholos tombs contained gold sculptures of owls.

Peacock. Though the peacock has, in common parlance, become associated with vanity, among other ills, it actually has a long sacred history. While its feathers were a symbol of the power of the sun, the bird was a sacred symbol of Hera and later, for the Romans, of Juno; peacocks wandered the temples of Hera. In India, where the peacock originated, the goddess Indra sat on a peacock throne, while Sarasvati rode a peacock. The Muslims consider the peacock a symbol of the cosmos, or the sun and the moon. Even early Christian symbolism preserves some of the sacred tradition connected to peacocks: the depiction of two peacocks drinking from a single chalice signified spiritual rebirth, while the "eyes" of the peacock feathers stood for divine omniscience.

Phoenix. A purely mythological creature laden with sacral meaning, the phoenix was said to rise from its own ashes after being consumed by fire; a variation on the myth has it taking place on the altar at Heliopolis. In ancient Egypt, the phoenix was known as Bennu; the renewed morning sun was Bennu reborn and was the soul of the sun god Ra and the living symbol of Osiris. Bennu's sanctuary was called the House of the Obelisk, and he was thought, as told in the *Book of the*

Dead, to enable the deceased to take on the form of the phoenix. The phoenix takes its name from the Greek for "crimson" and is a powerful symbol of resurrection or rebirth. In China, the phoenix is the fabulous *feng huang,* the emperor of all birds, the second among the four supernatural creatures (along with the dragon, the unicorn, and the tortoise). The phoenix was said to appear only when reason prevailed in the country and in times of peace and prosperity. It rules over the southern quadrant of the heavens and symbolizes the sun, as well as the warmth and bounty of summer. The phoenix is active in all matters of fertility, human and animal alike.

Try drawing your own vision of the phoenix and its wondrous rebirth; use it as emblem of spiritual change on your altar.

Pig or sow. From the agricultural Neolithic onward, the fast-growing and fecund sow has been associated with the feminine, specifically with the powers of growth and regeneration associated with the Earth Goddess. The pig was an important sacrificial animal on the islands of Malta and Crete, as well as in later Greek rituals sacred to Demeter and Artemis, including the Mysteries at Eleusis and the Thesmophoria. Freya, the Norse goddess, was also known as Syr (sow). Cerridwen, the goddess of the Celts, was a sow goddess. In ancient Egypt, a sow was the epiphany of the goddess Nut.

Raven. Sometimes associated with ill omen and death, the intelligent raven has long been associated with prophecy as well as with knowledge; in Greek myth, the raven was Apollo's companion, although the god turned the once-white bird coal black as punishment for the raven's betrayal of one of Apollo's secrets. In Norse myth, Odin's two ravens, Thought and Memory, bring him news of the human world each day; they also tell him where to find the magic cauldron Odhroerir. In Irish legend, gods and goddesses alike take the form of the raven on the battlefield. In the Old Testament, the prophet Elijah is fed by ravens, who bring him meat and bread in the desert. In Native American myths, the raven is a supernatural being and, in the Pacific Northwest, a hero, transformer, and trickster by turns, who is credited with bringing humanity forth out of a clamshell, stealing the sun for humankind, and creating the mountains, rivers, and lakes as well as other animals.

Snake. The Judeo-Christian depiction of the snake as evil incarnate is a comparatively recent revision of a long, sacred history that understood the snake as a symbol of primal, earth-bound energy, full of mystery and promise, and an intimate epiphany of the Goddess of life and death. Because the snake lives in the crevices of the earth, it is symbolic both of the earth's life force and the realm of the dead; in its hibernation and sloughing off of its skin, it also symbolizes rebirth. The coiling movement of the snake was understood as symbolic of the life force and energy, often rendered stylistically as a spiral.

Snakes were venerated in ancient Egypt and appear in the hands of gods and goddesses; the goddess Neith, the weaver associated with life and fate, was portrayed as a cobra, while Renenutet, the harvest deity of childbirth and nursing, had her epiphany as a snake. Minoan priestesses held snakes in their hands; Athena is portrayed with the whirl of snakes around her, indicative of her lineage from the ancient Earth Mother. For the Romans, the house snake epitomized the essential spirit or "Genius" of a male or the "Juno" of a woman. The symbolic importance of the snake in Native American traditions is underscored by the 4,000-year-old serpent mound, one-quarter-mile long, in Chillicothe, Ohio, whose ritual purpose is unknown. Many Native American tribes considered the cast-off snakeskin to contain potent magic.

Snakes, spirals, and serpentine forms will impart the feminine life force to your rituals and altars. Remember, as always, that your inclusion of the snake need not be a literal model; a coiled ribbon or a drawn spiral will serve equally well.

Spider. It is the spider's ability to spin and weave—both of which are acts with sacral overtones in many cultures—that lends it profound spiritual significance. In India, the spider's web is both a symbol of creativity and, with its center point placed within a spiral, an image of the cosmos; it is Maya, the weaver of the web of illusion, who is associated with the spider. Just as other symbols pertaining to spinning and weaving are metaphors for the transitory quality of life, so too is the spider's web, associated with the moon and its phases. The Mayan lunar goddess Ixcanleom is associated with the spider; among the Native American peoples, Spider Woman was a creatrix.

Use images of the spider and its web on your altar to signify the mystery of life.

Swan. The graceful swan has long been associated with prophecy, a gift that the swan obtained by being present at Apollo's birth and carrying him across the sky; the swan was an epiphany of the god and his music, particularly because of the ancient legend recounting how the swan sang exquisitely at the moment of death. Swans were also sacred to the Goddess, according to Robert Graves, because of their whiteness and their flight in a **V**-pattern (a female symbol).

Thunderbird. A supernatural creature of Native American culture, the thunderbird, as its name implies, created the thunder in the sky by flapping its wings and lightning by opening or closing its eyes. An extremely powerful creature, capable of conferring great blessings as well as creating both war and discord, the thunderbird was addressed as "Our Grandfathers" in Algonquian dialects. As a rain bringer, the thunderbird was especially sacred to the Indians of the arid Southwest.

Tiger. In China, the tiger is chief among the land animals, the terrestrial correspondent to the dragon of the waters, and is a protector spirit so powerful that the Chinese did not call it by name but by special euphemistic formulae. The tiger is the essence of the female principle, *yin*.

It is thought to be a special terror to demons and malignant spirits, and thus images of tigers were placed both on gravestones and in and over doorways of both domestic and sacred space. The god of wealth is often represented as a tiger. On Tibetan prayer flags, the tiger is always shown in contest with the dragon, and five tigers, each of a different color, are thought to be a mystical representation of the five elements: the center yellow tiger, the earth; the upper-right blue one, wood; the red lower-right one, fire; the upper-left black one, water; the lower-left one, metal.

Tortoise, or turtle. For the Chinese one of the four spiritually endowed animals, the tortoise is an emblem of strength, longevity, and endurance; it is associated with the direction north, winter, and the color black. The tortoise is an attendant of P'an Ku, who carved the universe out of blocks of granite with a chisel and a mallet. Both the Chinese and the Hindus saw the tortoise as a symbol of the universe: its shell represented the vault of the sky, while its belly was the earth that moves on the waters. Its longevity made it eternal like the universe. The wood columns of the Temple of Heaven were said to rest on the backs of tortoises to ensure the wood's eternality. In China and then later Japan, the shell of the turtle was used for divination. The shell was first pierced and then placed in a fire; new cracks in the shell would provide the answers to the priest's and king's questions.

In other cultures as well, the turtle is a symbol of the universe: the Hindus pictured a turtle on which an elephant stood supporting the world, while the Delaware Indians thought that the World Tree grew out of the turtle's back.

Wolf. Once seen as a marauder and predator in the European tradition, in contemporary times the wolf has become an important symbol of the wilderness spirit. The ancient Greeks understood it as a ghost animal, while the Romans, who considered the wolf sacred to Mars, thought the appearance of a wolf was a portent of victory in battle. In Native American traditions, the wolf is an important spirit teacher and clan animal.

Set upon an antique obi decorated with pine trees and flying cranes, this gratitude altar includes a traditional Thai spirit house painted in gold paint and set all over with bits of brightly colored glass as well as a statue of Kuan Yin, the Chinese goddess of compassion. The large white-and-pink conch is there to call the spirits in thanks; the shells stand for the pilgrimage that is life. The beautiful tulips are an offering of thanks for the gift of spring that is only a month or so away.

Offerings

The practice of making offerings to the supernatural deities is probably as old as the idea of sacred space itself. The word *sacrifice* is from the Latin, meaning "to make holy," and the very act of sacrifice or offering that is made to a god or goddess makes that which is offered holy. Whether we understand the ancient practice of animal sacrifice as an act that was meant to restore the spirit of the beast to the supernatural realm, or as an act of thanksgiving or perhaps appeasement, nonetheless we know from the carefully arranged bear skulls on an altar and in wall niches in the Swiss cave of Drachenloch that blood offerings are at least 50,000 years old. In Western culture, they form a part of the tradition that continued through the Old Testament, as outlined in Leviticus.

Bloodless sacrifice is probably just as ancient, and both appear to have been part of ritual from the very beginning of humanity's awareness of the spirit. Thus, at the Maltese temple of Tarxien, dating from the fourth millennium, in addition to bones of animals, heaps of real shells as well as clay models were found near the altars and fireplaces, while at the cave of Psychro on Crete, a place of ritual dating from 3000 B.C.E., there is evidence of animal bones, ash, cups filled with vegetative matter, and amulets offered in ceremony.

Offerings perform a variety of functions in cultures all over the world. In addition to propitiating or thanking a supernatural, they serve as well—by the very act of making holy—to energize a sacred place or bring the deity's presence into it. All over the world, in ancient and contemporary times, food and foodstuffs continue to be important offerings. In ancient Egypt, in addition to the copious offerings left in the public temples, the home chapel with an image of a god was gifted each day; near the granary or winepress, wine and flowers were presented to Renenutet, the goddess of harvest. Similarly, in contemporary Thailand as well as other places Thais have settled, the spirit house—the abode of the kitchen god—receives a daily offering of food and water in thanks so that he, in turn, can offer sustenance to those who need it. The Greeks honored and propitiated Hecate at the full or new moon by leaving her circular cakes topped with candles in a ritual known as the Supper of Hecate. Similarly, in Tibetan Buddhism, each day the Buddha is gifted with the essential daily offerings: flowers, incense, sacred cakes, rice, water, light, and music.

Offerings or gifts continue to be part of contemporary rituals because the act of offering signifies our willingness and our intention to be present and to open up our spirits. Natural objects of beauty—flowers, fruits, and shells—are used by many people on their altars; others feel that the offering should be a cherished object. Nancy Blair likes to bring gifts that have been found—the heart-shaped rocks that wash up on the beach where she lives or a beautiful shell. For group rituals, offering up something of each of ourselves is a way of connecting, as is offering food and drink that is intended to be shared after the end of the ritual. Tending and maintaining the altar and the offerings placed on it is, for many people—as it has been through the millennia—an important part of spiritual awareness. In gifting, we learn giving.

Once again, the descriptions of offerings on the following pages are meant to inspire you rather than to be prescriptive. Discovering that so many offerings—food, salt, and flowers among them—are common to the different spiritual practices of peoples all over our planet has made me focus on the underlying oneness of the human experience.

Ashes. Although, on the one hand, ashes symbolize the transitory nature of life and thus signify mourning in many cultures, ancient and contemporary, on the other, as the residue of fire that was thought to contain the concentrated power of the object burned, ashes are also potent and magical. The Navajo believe that ashes offer protection against evils and thus use them for rites of exorcism; used before sunrise, ashes, like pollen, scatter the evils of the night. Ashes have been used to purify altars and other sacral objects since ancient times. The Greeks connected purification by fire with regeneration, following the model of the Phoenix that arose from the ashes of the fire that consumed it. In Greece as elsewhere, ashes were sprinkled over fields as the agents of renewal to ensure the growth of the crops. In Tibet, images of Buddha made of the ashes of holy men and clay are fashioned to drive away demons in honor of Darma Rajah. In Taoist ritual, messages are sent to the gods by burning them; the wafting smoke of the incense burned with them is thought to take the messages to the heavenly presences. In ancient times, the Taoist priest would consume the ashes, for, in doing so, he would release the gods within himself who would then communicate with the gods without.

See also "Fire," page 91, and "Smoke," page 92.

Blood. In ancient times, blood and life were virtually synonymous; thus, blood was important to the magic and rituals of many religions the world over. Blood was thought to contain the essence, or spirit, of the being, and so by drinking the blood of a god or an object made holy by the act of sacrifice, the worshiper took on his spirit. The medieval legend of the Holy Grail underscores the symbolic properties of blood that were preserved in Christianity. The Grail was said to be the dish used by Christ at the Last Supper; at the Crucifixion, Joseph of Arimathea took the Grail and collected some of Christ's blood in it. According to legend, he took the Grail to England, where it disappeared because of the unworthiness and impurity of its guardians.

The life-endowing qualities of blood were also imitated in ritual: for thousands of years, the dead were covered with red ocher and surrounded by emblems of life such as the triangle and the cowrie shell, and runes were colored red to give them life. In Taoist rituals, newly carved statues of gods are consecrated by "opening their eyes," that is, by marking them with drops of blood or red paint.

Blood sacrifice was a rite of renewal or restoration and could also be either an act of tribute or placation of a deity. Specific animals were offered in sacrifice and the blood caught in a vessel and then poured on the altar. Symbolic substitutes for blood—wines, red-colored liquids, and paints—are used similarly to sanctify a sacred place. Even our English word *blessing* connects to the historical importance of blood as a symbol of life in ritual, for it comes from the Old English, meaning to "make holy with blood."

Corn. In Native American traditions, corn is the staple food as well as an important part of rite, offering, and sacrifice and is known in the many different languages of the continent as "Our Mother" or "Our Life." Corn was part of a complex mythology that varied in detail from one people to another, but overall it was the emblem of the all-giving quality of nature, at once a symbol of the One and of the Many. Corn was associated with the six directions: red corn with the north, blue with the east, black with the south, and yellow with the west. White corn was the direction of upward; variegated corn was the direction of the underworld. Among the Navajo, cornmeal—white for males, yellow for females—was a part of many rituals, including sandpainting. Corn pollen, too, was a sacral essence: prayers began with a bit of pollen touched to the lips and then thrown to the Sky and the Sun.

Grain. The sacred fruit of earth that yields bread, the staff of life, wheat, and other grains—from the earliest days of agriculture—was among the most important gifts humanity had to offer its deities. Grain was an emblem of the Earth Mother, and statues from the

Neolithic actually have grain pressed into the clay. For ancient Egyptians and Greeks alike, the paradox of the grain—it needs to be cut down or symbolically killed in order to grow again—illuminated the mysteries of life, as well as the eternal cycle. Thus, the slain Osiris was shown with wheat sprouting from his body, while, at Eleusis, an ear of wheat was an epiphany of the ancient mysteries of Demeter and Persephone. The eternal promise of renewal embodied in the grain even illuminates Christianity, for, in the Gospel of John, Christ says, "Except a corn of wheat fall into the ground, it abideth alone; but if it die, it bringeth forth much fruit."

Grinding the grain was a sacral activity, as was baking it and turning it into bread in cultures the world over; as the gift of the gods, bread or cake was an important part of harvest and firstfruits rituals, as well as an offering to specific deities, either burned on an altar or ritually consumed. As early as the Neolithic, as Marija Gimbutas has pointed out, clay seals were used to stamp specific designs on bread used as offerings; shrines dating from 5000 B.C.E. often have miniature bread ovens contained within them. Special cakes were offered to the goddess Inanna, symbols of the harvest of her body, which would then be ritually consumed by the worshipers, her "children." In ancient Rome, *mola salsa,* a cake made of wheat gathered, roasted, ground, mixed with salt, and then baked by the vestal virgins, was offered on the altar before every sacrifice.

In the Old Testament, bread symbolizes God's care of his people, and, in Judaism, bread is gifted with a special grace after a meal, thanking God, he "who brings forth bread from the ground." On the Sabbath, the bread is covered so as to spare it embarrassment, for the blessing for the bread is shorter than that for the candles. Bread's sacral import shows itself clearly in Christian ritual as well: Christ identifies himself as "the bread of life," and, at the Last Supper, bread symbolizes his sacrifice upon the Cross.

Honey. The fruit of the earth and the air, gathered by the winged bees from the flowers, honey is a sacral food in many cultures, used as an offering or propitiation to the gods and goddesses, a sacrifice, or food for the dead. Its sweetness made it a symbol of all gifts. As one of the first known preservatives, honey was also connected to magic and rebirth, for it was used to embalm the dead as early as ancient Egypt. The bee and, thus, its harvest, honey, were associated with the moon, and because of the ancient understanding that bees were born out of the carcasses of dead bulls, the bull as well. In ancient Crete, according to Anne Baring and Jules Cashford, honey was an important part of rituals that celebrated the rising of the Dog Star, Sirius, and the New Year. Forty days before the rising of the Dog Star, honey was ritually collected in darkness and then fermented into a mead drink that was part of ecstatic rituals. According to the *Odyssey* and the *Oresteia*, honey mixed with water or milk, was a libation for the dead, as well as the food for the gods (Zeus himself was fed it), and thus part of offerings left at temples; the serpent guardian of the Acropolis was fed a honey cake each month.

In other cultures and in other ages, honey was an equally important part of religious and sacral activities. In Hindu myth, the Asvin twins brought honey to the world, and the faithful were fed honey from an ever-flowing stream. In the Old Testament, the words of the prophets are "as sweet as honey"; when combined with milk (*see Milk*), honey has even more meaning, for the promised land is the land "of milk and honey." Even so, the strength of pagan associations with honey as an offering made it the subject of an injunction contained in Leviticus 2:11, where the Jews were specifically forbidden to offer it.

In China, the kitchen god, or god of the hearth, Tsao-wang, was propitiated by offering him sweetmeats with honey or by rubbing honey onto the lips of the statue on the kitchen altar; since, in addition to apportioning the length of life to each member of the household and bestowing wealth or poverty, Tsao-wang also reported on the virtues and vices of the household, the stickiness of the honey was meant to assure that, when he got to heaven, he would be unable to open his lips.

Milk. It is the first food, the primal food, of all humans; as a symbol, milk resonates with the miracle of life and its sustenance and of the birth-giving and nurturance of the divine feminine. Like the waters and the rains, milk is a divine moisture, and it pours equally from the breasts of the Great Mother of the Neolithic, incised with snakes, and meanders, as it does from those of the suckling Egyptian Isis, the Greek Hera, and the Virgin Mary. Not surprisingly, milk was associated with the moon. In Christianity, milk is a symbol of spiritual sustenance, associated in Catholicism with the Virgin Mary.

When combined with milk, honey has even more sacral overtones, for both are completely of nature, pure at their inception, and can be consumed without any preparation.

Olive and olive oil. The fruit of the olive tree, the oil that is pressed from it, and the tree itself, known to the Mediterranean since the Neolithic, have a long sacral history. Offerings of olives have been found in Minoan Crete, while, in Greece, the tree was sacred to both Athena and Apollo. The live olive tree was a symbol of continuity and vitality, as well as wisdom and restraint. The olive branch was an emblem of the peace bringer, as it would continue to be through the Judeo-Christian era as a sign of the renewed and constant covenant of God.

Olive oil, which burns slowly and relatively smokelessly, burned for thousands of years in sanctuaries, temples, and votives, as well as in the lamps of the people. In the ancient world, the act of anointing another with olive oil was a mark of respect for the living and the dead alike. Sacred stones and places were also anointed with the oil of the olive, an act that both sacralized and transformed at once, as it continues to through the present day. The omphalos at Delphi, the spiritual center of ancient Greece, was anointed with oil, as is the sacred black rock at Mecca today. In the Old Testament, when Jacob had his vision of angels, he set up the stone that he had used as his pillow, poured oil on it, and called it Beth-El, or "House of the Lord." When Moses had the Tabernacle built at Sinai, everything in it was anointed with oil, as both temples and churches are today.

Rice. As important to forms of worship and ritual in the East as grain and bread were in the West, rice provides the primary sustenance for more than half the population of the world. Rice was placed in the mouths of the dead to feed them and piled high in bowls for ancestral worship. In Japan, the goddess Amaterasu is honored as the bringer of rice, as is the god Inari, or the "rice bearer"; in Thailand, the rice goddess is Maeae Posop, and each grain of rice is thought to contain some of her soul. A food of the spirit, often described in kinship terms, rice is the second part of the world in Buddhism, after Buddha himself. Rice is also a symbol of fecundity in many places in the world, from the Hindu marriage ceremony to the Western, where rice is also thrown over the couple.

Salt. Perhaps, along with water, the most important offering in ritual, salt is a potent symbol of immortality and resurrection (since meats, cured with salt, did not spoil, and salt was used to embalm the dead), as well as an ancient agent of purification. (Such was the power of salt, though, that too much of it could leave the land barren, a tactic practiced by the Romans against their vanquished enemies.) Salt had magical powers that offered protection against demons: the ancient Romans rubbed salt on the lips of infants to protect them, a practice echoed in Christian baptism, which sometimes includes placing crystals of salt in the child's mouth. Altars in ancient Egypt, Greece, and Rome were ritually cleansed with salt, perhaps taking the place of blood, just as Christian churches and their sacral artifacts would be later on in history. In the Old Testament, salt is a symbol of God's covenant, while in the New Testament, Christ called his disciples "the salt of the earth." Among the Native Americans, who gathered salt in ritual ceremony, Salt Mother was a benevolent mother goddess, also associated with rain; she is sometimes identified as Changing Woman's sister, and she and her gift—salt—were thought to endow strength and endurance.

Salt has special resonance because it is both of the earth and of the waters; we are reminded of the great plenty and life-giving nature of the ocean's waters, the salty taste of blood, and the amniotic fluid in which we all come to life.

Tobacco. The sacred plant of the Americas, tobacco plays an important role in Native American rituals and is often used as an offering as well. Origin stories from many tribes attest to the mystical nature of this plant, which is native to our continent. The tobacco pouch is a ceremonial object, often portrayed in Navajo sandpainting and sometimes used in lieu of prayer sticks; both Sun and Moon possess tobacco pouches themselves. Smoke offerings of tobacco are made to the Great Spirit; the whorls of smoke take messages to the god, while at the same time, the participant in the ceremony inhales the smoke, sending his spirit upward along with the messages. The smoking of the pipe—itself a ritual object—is a way of communicating with the spirit world. Tobacco is used for invoking the six directions (the four cardinal points plus up and down) and for assuring harvest and abundance as well as in rites pertaining to peace and war.

Water. Consecrated, or holy, waters are part of ritual the world over. The altar in Tibetan Buddhism always has, on its lower tier, a spouted water jug for filling bowls for water offerings; the water is sometimes tinged with saffron or perfumed. In Tibet, the rising of the Dog Star, Sirius, in September is heralded by a water festival of thanksgiving in which springs and rivers are gifted with rites and offerings.

Our contemporary understanding that all living things depend on water—the rains, the rivers and streams, and the oceans—makes the use of water on our altars even more spiritually potent.

Wine. Long before Christianity identified the fruit of the grape with the blood of Christ, wine was known as the blood of life and was associated with religion and the spirit. In ancient Egypt, dark grapes were called the "eyes of Horus." Wine could break magical spells and reveal the truth and was suitable as a libation for the dead, poured directly onto the earth. Sacred to the Greek Dionysus, god of the grape, wine signified blood and sacrifice, as well as youth and eternal life.

The Tree of Life: Boughs and Leaves

Roots are the branches down in the earth.
Branches are roots in the air.

RABINDRANATH TAGORE

The trees that reached from the earth high into the heavens were at the beginning, as they are now, places of refuge as well as majesty; they seemed, like the birds who perched amid their branches, to be able to mediate between earth and sky, here and there, above and below. Their roots made them equally a part of the underworld and the earth and the heavens; the tree alone spanned the three realms. It is no wonder that individual trees as well as groves and stands of them became sacred places of rite and sometimes divination, originally identified with the Earth Mother and later other deities as well. The tree may have been humanity's first altar, or high place. It was in the form of the sycamore that the Egyptian Hathor fed the souls of dead. The Goddess on Crete was worshiped in groves of trees at sanctuaries on mountain peaks; the priestesses at Dodona in Greece foretold the future under the branches of a sacred oak. In Sumer, the tree belonged to Dumuzi, or Tammuz, god of vegetation. At Ephesus, sacred to Artemis, the statue of the goddess, nine feet tall, loomed treelike over her worshipers; as the Tree of Life, breastlike figs, as well as bees and vines, cover her body. It was under the fig tree that Buddha reached enlightenment. In some Native American cultures, the tree was considered so sacred that live trees were not felled; if it was necessary to cut one down, rituals celebrating the tree's gift of life to the tribe would be held.

Trees that shed their leaves and then regain them in the spring are symbolic of renewal; evergreens—the cypress, the palm, and the fir—epitomize the eternal and the everlasting. Thus pine and cypress trees were planted near burial places to strengthen the souls of the dead with their vitality. Sap, the life force of the tree, was considered a divine essence. So powerful was the tree in the human imagination that many mythologies incorporate the idea of a world tree, one that literally sits at the center of the cosmos.

Because the parts of the tree, its boughs and twigs, were also sacred and possessed of magical properties, wands, staffs, and prayer sticks made from specific trees—the willow in the Celtic tradition and the spruce in the Native American—were thought to be especially holy. Nut-bearing trees are specifically associated with knowledge. Runic symbols used in divination, reported by Tacitus in the first century C.E., acquired some of their power from the tree they were made of; the branch of a nut-bearing tree was cut into strips and a symbol inscribed on each. The strips were tossed onto a white cloth, and, after prayer, the priest choose three at random and then prophesied.

For an outside altar, a tree can provide shade and shelter, as well as a guardian spirit. (For more, see page 194.) Following the ancient traditions, a tree can actually become an altar. One of the most marvelous examples of this I've seen was a tree that members of my community decorated with handwritten prayer flags and found objects strung on wire—beads, buttons, bottle caps, discarded parts of toys and trinkets—under the tutelage of the artist Sarah Teofanov.

Using fallen parts of trees—leaves, branches, fruits—on your altar can energize your rituals. The oak's acorn, for example, which only appears after twenty years' growth, is a perfect symbol of the future and potential and can be used to focus a meditation; pinecones, with their intricate pattern of petals, are a visual reminder of the oneness amid complexity. For a winter solstice celebration, Nancy Blair placed pine boughs on her outdoor altar and strewed the fallen pine needles on the path that led to it. As she walked down the path, she released their scent, invigorating her sacred space. Of course, when we bring the tree indoors, we are also reminded forcibly of our connection to nature and the greater world outside us.

Ash. In Greece, the ash was sacred to Poseidon, god of the waters, while in Norse myth, the mighty ash, Yggradsil, with its roots in the well of wisdom, was the world tree under which the gods conferred. For the Irish, according to Robert Graves, three of the five Magic Trees were ash and the source for the wands of the Druids. The strength and the power of the ash were legendary and thus, to confer might on a weapon, the shafts of spears were fashioned from it.

Cedar. Sacred to Osiris, the cedar was prized for its fragrance and used for coffins in ancient Egypt, partly because, like all conifers, it was evergreen and thus a symbol of immortality. Cedar was sacred to the Romans, who fashioned from it both statues of the gods and goddesses and torches, for the scent of the burning wood. Among certain Native American tribes, cedar was also valued for its scent and smudging properties.

Cypress. Sacred to many gods and goddesses, including Cronus, Apollo, Asclepius, Cybele, Persephone, Aphrodite, Artemis, Hera, Athena, as well as the Greek Fates and Furies, the cypress was associated with both generation and death. As a sacred wood, cypress was used by the Egyptians for mummy cases, while the Greeks buried their heroes in cypress caskets. In Japan, the *hinoki*—a variety of cypress— was used in Shinto worship; because it was pure, two sticks of *hinoki* were rubbed together to produce ritual fire.

Fig tree. A sacred tree, the fig is an emblem of life and plenty, for it exemplifies the union of the feminine—its fruit, the fig—with the masculine, its tri-lobed leaf. Sometimes called the "fruit of Heaven," the fig tree was sacred to Juno in Rome and was the tree under whose branches Buddha reached enlightenment.

Holly. Holly branches used as tokens of friendship were part of the Roman Saturnalia. For the Druids, it was a plant of death as well as re- generation, sacred to Hel, goddess of the underworld; the red berry of the plant was a symbol of the regenerative blood. The Druids used holly in their rites, and ordinary people used the power of the holly branch to protect their homes against evil spirits. The Zoroastrians of ancient Persia and India used an infusion of the leaves and berries in religious ceremonies.

Mistletoe. An evergreen semiparasitic plant with white berries that lives on deciduous trees, mistletoe was long regarded as sacred and magic, a protector as well as a bestower of life and, paradoxically, of death. The Greeks and Romans identified it as an herb of the underworld; in Norse myth, the god of peace, Baldur, was slain by an arrow of mistletoe. It was sacred to the Celtic Druids, who, on the sixth night of the moon, amid great ceremony, cut the mistletoe from its host, the oak, with a golden sickle. It was then, along with two white bulls, offered to the gods in sacrifice. Please note that mistletoe is toxic and should be kept away from children and domestic animals.

Myrtle. As a tree or shrub, myrtle was sacred to the goddesses Astarte and Aphrodite and, like other evergreens, was associated with immortality and rebirth. Myrtle was forbidden, though, at the ceremonies honoring Bona Dea, the Roman goddess of fertility and chastity.

Oak. The most sacred of all trees, the oak was thought by the ancient Greeks to be the first tree created, with roots that went down into the underworld. A symbol of immortality and endurance, the oak was sacred to Zeus at Dodona, where priestesses sat beneath its branches and prophesied. To bring rain, the priests would dip an oak branch into a sacred spring. At the Daedala, the festival of the renewed marriage of Zeus and Hera, images of the god and goddess were carved out of oak trees chosen by the auguries of ravens. They were then burned on an altar. At the shrine of Diana at Nemi, a perpetual fire, kept alight by vestal virgins, was fed by the wood of a sacred oak. Because of the long-held belief that the oak was struck by lightning more frequently than other trees, it was sacred to the thunder gods, Thor among them.

The oak was sacred to the Druids, the ancient Celtic priests and priestesses, who worshiped in groves of oak alongside rivers or other bodies of water. They ate the acorns of the oak before prophesying.

The age-old association of the oak with holiness survived through the nineteenth century in England with the tradition of the "Gospel oaks," under which clergy and parishioners gathered to read the Gospels and to ask for God's blessings.

Palm. Egyptians laid the fronds of palms on coffins, for the date palm was sacred to the goddess Hathor, who fed the souls of the dead. The Greeks and the Romans regarded the palm as a symbol of triumph (the Greek Nike, goddess of victory, held a palm branch in her hand), an association that, in the Christian context, became emblematic of Christ's victory over death. The palm tree was, according to Robert Graves, the Tree of Life in the Babylonian story of paradise lost; it was also sacred to Astarte, Isis, and Aphrodite. The Greek word for palm, *phoenix,* connects it both to fire and the sun, as well as to rebirth.

Pine. For the Chinese and Japanese, the pine tree epitomizes the life force; in Japan, its wood is used in the building of Shinto temples as well as in ritual implements, and the tree itself is considered especially hospitable as a dwelling for divinities and spirits. The tree was also sacred to Cybele, and at ceremonies celebrating the death and rebirth of nature, the pine tree symbolized the body of Attis, Cybele's consort.

The pinecone, both masculine and feminine at once, was a phallic symbol and a sign of fecundity and abundance for the Greeks, the Etruscans, and the Romans. It was sacred to Artemis and Aphrodite, as well as to Dionysus. The pinecone also stood for immortality, as did the tree itself.

Poplar. Associated with the Earth Goddess, poplars grew at the mouth of Calypso's cave in the *Odyssey*. According to Robert Graves, white poplar was sacred to the Greek Persephone in her regenerative aspect. The two-color leaf was interpreted as symbolic of the sun and the moon, and also the world above and the underworld, as well as the dual nature of all things. Hercules wore a crown of poplar leaves while traveling to the underworld (the part of the leaf exposed to Hades turned black, while the part against his skin stayed light), and the poplar was sacred to him.

Spruce. Important to Navajo rituals were wands and brushes made from spruce branches, especially for the "Chant of the Sun's House."

Sycamore. Like the cedar, the sycamore was sacred to the Goddess of the Grain, Queen of the Earth, the Sumerian Inanna, and was her epiphany; to symbolize her presence, sycamores were planted in her temples.

Willow. In the Greco-Roman tradition, the willow was sacred to Hecate, Circe, Hera, and Persephone, often in the death aspects of the goddesses; at the same time, though, willow was connected to creativity (the virgin willow goddess Helice gave her name to the Helicon, home to the nine Muses), as well as to Apollo, god of poetry and prophecy. Because the willow needs a great deal of water and therefore grows near it, it was also lunar in nature. According to Robert Graves, the willow is associated both with fertility rites and witchcraft. The Chinese goddess of mercy, Kuan Yin, sprinkles the waters of life from her long-necked vase with a willow wand. Among the Prairie Indians, the willow was a symbol of seasonal rebirth.

Yew. As an evergreen, the yew was symbolic of immortality, although it had very strong connections as well to the gods and goddesses of the underworld. It was sacred to Hecate and, in Rome, yew wreathes adorned the black bulls sacrificed in her honor. Like the oak, the yew takes many years to reach maturity and is especially long-lived, so it stood for endurance and strength. In the Celtic tradition, the yew is a funerary tree; thought to be poisonous (the tips of spears were dipped in crushed yew berries), the yew is one of the five magical trees of Ireland, according to Robert Graves's *The White Goddess,* symbolic of the death aspect of the Irish triple goddess.

Herbs and Spices

Herbs and spices, as the offspring of the sacred earth, have long been important to ritual and ceremony. As humanity's first pharmacopoeia, herbs were considered powerful healers as well as magical in essence and had wide use as amulets against evil spirits. They could be strewn on altars as gifts either to propitiate the gods and goddesses or to protect the celebrant. Dried and ground, they impart scent, color, and flavoring and have been used to sacralize waters in ceremonies the world over. Agents of purification, they have been part of ritual cleansing for thousands of years, used strewn or burned in cultures all over the world, from Europe and the Far East to North America. Old herbals, as well as surviving traditions in Native America and elsewhere, reveal that the harvesting of herbs was often conducted with rites and ceremonies that honored the plant being gathered. A sermon by Saint Elroy, preached in A.D. 640 in England, makes it clear that the old ways of honoring the herbs of the earth survived the first centuries of Christianity, for he exhorted Christians not "to make lustrations nor to enchant herbs." The existence of prayers dedicated to the gathering of herbs from the twelfth and thirteenth centuries underscore the fact that the old ways of honoring Earth died hard.

Bringing herbs out of our kitchens and into our sacred spaces is one way of reclaiming our connection to the bounty of earth. You can use herbs in many ways on your altar—as symbols (rosemary for remembrance or sage for wisdom) or as offerings, for scenting or for smudging.

Remember, if you are burning or smudging herbs, use caution and common sense. Make sure your herbs or bundle are in a fireproof receptacle and that the surface beneath the receptacle is protected. *Do not leave any burning substance*—herbs or candles—unattended. When burning herbs, take special care to make sure that the fire is actually out before leaving the sacred space; herbs will continue to smolder.

See also Resources and Bibliography on pages 208 and 211.

Basil. In India, basil is sacred to Vishnu and Lakshmi and grown near homes and temples as protection. The dead were buried with basil leaves, for they were said to open the gates of heaven to the pious. In Christian legend, basil is said to have grown up around Christ's tomb, and so, in the Greek Orthodox Church, it is set in pots around the altar and used for holy water.

Bay. The laurel is sacred to Apollo, god of prophecy, poetry, and healing, and so the oracle at Delphi put a bay leaf between her lips before prophesying. Considered a protective herb, capable of warding off evil or malevolent spirits, it was often incorporated into the roofs of temples; in ancient Rome, priests used laurel twigs to sprinkle sacral liquids such as blood and water.

Frankincense. Culturally familiar to most of us as one of the gifts of the Magi to the infant Jesus, frankincense was, from ancient times onward, one of the chief burnt offerings to the gods in ancient Greece, Rome, Persia, Babylon, and Assyria. In Jewish tradition, frankincense was part of the ceremonial incense and one of the offerings on the Sabbath.

Garlic. Garlic was a talisman against evil in many cultures, as the more recent vampire legends indicate. The Egyptians swore oaths upon it; the Greeks left it as an offering to propitiate Hecate at the crossroads. The Romans associated garlic with Mars, the god of war, and ate it to increase their strength and endurance before going into battle.

Hyssop. Taking its name from the Greek for "holy herb," hyssop was long used to cleanse and purify holy places. In the Old Testament, hyssop was used in lustral waters.

Parsley. Sacred to the dead in Greece and Rome, parsley was said to have sprung up from the blood of the hero Archemorus; it was also a sign of victory.

Rosemary. Romans crowned their household gods with rosemary; they believed it could ward off evil and thus burned rosemary incense as a purifying element. From Greek times forward, rosemary has been associated with remembrance; students would wear sprigs of rosemary to improve their memories. This particular herb is also closely associated with the Virgin Mary, for it is said a bush of rosemary sheltered her and her child on the flight into Egypt. In thanks, she turned the herb's flower blue.

Rue. Long used as a strewing herb, rue was thought by the Greeks and the Romans to offer protection against evil spirits, a reputation that continued up through the Middle Ages, when the herb was considered effective against the magic of djinn and pixies. Its name comes from the Greek *reuo,* meaning to "set free." In Christian symbolism, rue is the herb of repentance.

Saffron. Costly saffron, the dried orange-colored stamens of the autumn crocus, was prized by the Greeks and Romans and was used to cleanse as well as scent. In India, the gift of offering fruits, foods, and spices at Hindu temples is marked by the giver's receiving on the forehead a daub of saffron paste with a few grains of rice to symbolize goodness. Saffron is also an emblem of purity and humility, which is why the robes of Buddhist monks are dyed with saffron.

Sage. The sacred herb of the Romans, sage was gathered with ceremony, and the earth from which it was plucked was thanked with gifts of bread and wine. It can be used to symbolize wisdom and long life. Among the Native Americans, sage is prized for its cleansing properties when smudged.

Sunflower. Sunflowers were a sacred plant for the Incas, whose priestesses were adorned with sunflowers made of beaten gold. As its name indicates, this herb is a plant of the sun. Its seeds were an important part of Incan ritual.

Sweet grass. Dried and braided, sweet grass is used for smudging by Native Americans in many rites and ceremonies, including those of the sweat lodge. According to Brooke Medicine Eagle in *Buffalo Woman Comes Singing,* smudging with sweet grass is a "prayer for sweetness and goodness in one's life and surroundings."

Thyme. Its name, from the Greek "to burn a sacrifice," tells us that thyme was used as holy incense, thought to invigorate an altar. The Romans identified thyme as an aphrodisiac and sacrificed it to Venus, the goddess of love. Thyme was also thought to increase energy and bravery by the Greeks and Romans, an association that persisted through the Middle Ages.

Vervain. Sacred in many cultures, vervain was identified in Egypt with the tears of Isis; in ancient Greece, it was used to clean the altar of Zeus. Temple priests tucked the roots of vervain in their robes. The Romans grew vervain as altar plants for purification, as did the Druids, who also used vervain in their lustral waters to aid in visions and divination. Like mistletoe, another sacred plant, vervain was harvested by the Druids under holy strictures: it was gathered with the left hand in spring at the rising of the Dog Star, Sirius, when neither the moon nor the sun was visible. After the harvest, the Druids poured honey into the earth as compensation for the gift. In Persia, vervain is the herb of prophecy, while in Christian churches, it was used in holy water.

Yarrow. We know that yarrow has been known to humanity for many millennia, since fossilized yarrow pollen was found in Neanderthal burial caves. It is an herb with a powerful reputation for healing: it got its Latin name, *Achillea millefolum,* because Achilles was said to have stopped the bleeding of his troops with it. The ancient Chinese system of divination, the *I Ching,* was originally composed of fifty stalks of dried yarrow. Yarrow was also used by the Druids in rites and ceremonies.

....

Three altar niches sit side by side on a shelf in Marilyn Goldman's living room. Marilyn has painted and hand-decorated each of the altars, providing an evocative setting for the wide variety of sacred imagery she has collected from all over the world. In one, a vividly painted Ganesha—in brilliant reds, yellows, and blues—sits next to a mermaid, surrounded by fish. In another, a lovely Virgin of Guadelupe is framed by images of good and evil, an angel and a devil. In the last, two angels and a kachina remind us of the power of the spirit world. These small-scale altars, available from Altar Your Life, are a way of creating personal sacred space when there is little room to spare.

Fruits and Flowers

Why fruits and flowers have, for millennia, graced altars of every kind the world over requires little explanation. As gifts of the Earth Mother, their beauty and scent made them ready emblems of the divine, often, though not always, feminine in nature. One Minoan seal shows priestesses bearing gifts of ripe figs and water lilies, while another depicts the Goddess descending as three dancing priestesses invoke her amid a field of lilies. In ancient Greece, at Hera's temple in Argos, her priestesses gathered lilies of the valley and garlanded the altar. The original deities of Rome were guardians of the land, worshiped without images at the crossroads where four properties met; each property had a sacrificial altar to honor the guardian, or *lares*. Each December, the *lares* would be honored with sacrifices, while the boundary stones were garlanded with flowers. Later, in imperial times, there was an indoor altar to the household *lares* as well, who would be similarly honored and propitiated with fire, flowers, and bread. Roman worshipers tossed roses into the chariot bearing the sacred statue of Cybele, just as Catholics the world over honor the Virgin Mary with single blossoms and bouquets in churches and shrines alike.

Wreathes or garlands of flowers carry their own, intensified meaning, because their circular form symbolizes permanence, combined with the life force of the flower. Thus, from ancient times forward, flowers and wreathes have been associated with funerary rites and remembrances.

Fruits and flowers put us in touch with the great cycle of life of which they are a part and inform our own spirits. When Sarah Teofanov built a mourning altar to honor her friend Scott Fisher, a renowned mountain climber who died on Mount Everest, she used both flower petals and fresh cut flowers. Over the month-long period the altar was in place, it was tended but permitted to go through its own cycles of change and transformation. The flowers faded and died and then went to seed. One morning, Sarah came downstairs and realized that the seed pods of the flowers had burst—an epiphany of the life cycle renewing itself once more. She knew at that moment that the altar could now be dismantled.

Apple. While history has maligned the apple as the forbidden fruit (based on the similarity of the Latin words for "evil" and "apple"), in older traditions the apple was sacred, often associated with the feminine. When an apple is cut on the transverse, it contains a five-pointed star at its center, a symbol of the feminine and of Aphrodite. Greek myth recounts that Mother Earth gave Hera an apple as a wedding present; for the Norse, the apples of immortality were closely guarded by the goddess Idun. Celtic tradition connects this fruit to ancestral wisdom.

Cherry. In China, the cherry is the symbol of immortality, as the apple is in other cultures. The goddess Hsi-Wang Mu guarded the cherries of immortality that only ripened once every thousand years. The wood of the cherry tree was thought to have great power to dispel evil spirits, so the guardians of the doorway were traditionally carved of cherry wood.

Chrysanthemum. In the Orient, the chrysanthemum is the emblem of midautumn, a symbol of joviality, and a traditional offering flower. According to the *Penguin Dictionary of Symbols,* it is also, with its many petals, a solar symbol representing fullness and completion.

Daisy. Because it closes up at night and has a bright yellow center, the daisy, a symbol of innocence, takes its name from the Old English *daeges ege,* or "day's eye." In Christian tradition, it is sacred both to Mary Magdalene, for it was said to have sprung from her tears, and to Saint John.

Fig. The fig was a gift to the goddess of Minoan Crete, as ancient seals tell us, and has been called, in different cultures, "the fruit of heaven." The fig tree and its fruit were sacred to Artemis and to the Roman Juno Caprotina.

Grape. See "Wine," page 147.

Iris. The namesake flower of the goddess of the rainbow and the communicating spirit between heaven and earth, or the "eye of heaven," the iris symbolizes conciliation and joining.

Lily. Sacred to the Cretan goddess Britomartis, and later to Hera and Juno, the lily was a powerful symbol of the feminine and could be given as an offering to honor a goddess or to invoke her presence. It was said that the same milk that spilled from Hera's breasts as she suckled Heracles and created the Milky Way created the lily on earth; in ancient Rome, the flower was called *rosa Junonis* (Juno's rose). In Christian symbolism, the lily signified purity, and it is especially connected to the Virgin Mary and the Annunciation.

Lotus. Perhaps the flower with the oldest and most important spiritual meanings, the lotus was sacred in ancient Egypt as well as in China and Japan; it is the sacred flower of Buddhism and Hinduism. In Egypt, the lotus was a symbol of the rising sun and thus of the resurrection of the sun god Horus; it was an important offering and was re-created in sculpted and painted forms in tombs and other funerary artifacts. Because the lotus grew in the waters of the life-giving Nile, it represented fertility; its bud stood for all potential. Even before Buddhism reached China, the lotus was an emblem of summer, purity, and fruitfulness, symbolizing both spirit and creative power.

In Hindu myth, Lakshmi, the goddess of agriculture, is associated with the lotus, which is itself a symbol of the yoni, the female generative organ, or the womb of creation. In the creation story, while Vishnu lies sleeping on the waters, a single lotus emerges from his navel on which Brahma, the Creator, is seated. The lotus therefore is an emblem of all creation. The tree under which Buddha received his supreme enlightenment is often indicated by a lotus; as he attained compassion for all beings, he saw them as lotus stems in a lake, "some immersed in mud, others coming out of it, and still others beginning to blossom." He determined to bring them all to full bloom. The lotus, too, is an attribute of divinity, and thus, in the Hindu pantheon, deities are often shown seated on it. In Buddhism, too, the lotus is an important symbol: the Buddha is often seated on it or shown with it in his hand. On the sole of the Buddha's foot, it is one of the auspicious signs; it is also one of the emblems of good fortune.

The water lily, its leaves floating on the waters, its bud reaching skyward, is an extraordinary evocation of emergence. For incorporating the power of the water lily into your sacred space, see also "A Spiritual Oasis: The Water Garden," page 186.

Orange. The seeds that it contains make the orange an emblem of fertility. In China, the gift of twelve oranges at the New Year assures a year of happiness and prosperity.

Peach. Especially important in the Eastern cultures, the peach tree and its fruit are especially venerated because of their spiritual force (it was thought to have *ling,* or "soul substance"); in China, the peach is an emblem of long life and immortality. The spirit of the tree was so powerful that it was considered to have great powers in warding off evil; children wore peach-pit amulets around their necks for protection, while boughs from the tree protected the doorways of dwellings.

Pear. The pear tree was sacred to Hera, Aphrodite, and the Roman goddess of vegetation, Pomona, and the wood was often used for statues of the goddesses. In China, the pear is a symbol of longevity.

Peony. The genus name of the peony—*paeonia*—reveals its long association with the powers of healing, as well as magic; in Greek myth, Paeon was the physician to the gods and a student of Asclepius, god of healing. Both the whole plant and its seeds were thought to offer protection against demons, the spirits of the night, and natural disasters such as storms and shipwrecks.

In China, the peony is highly prized; the tree peony is the flower of the *yang* principle, as well as the sign of spring in the floral calendar.

Pomegranate. A fruit with many sacral and mystical associations, the pomegranate is feminine in essence and thus sacred to many goddesses, including Astarte, Demeter, Aphrodite, and Hera, who is often depicted with a pomegranate in her hand. Its many seeds were an emblem of fertility and of the womb, particularly because of the blood-red color of its juice and pulp. There is evidence to suggest that the pomegranate may have been part of the Mysteries at Greece's Eleusis.

I am particularly drawn to this fruit because of its essential mystery: its exterior yields no clues to what lies hidden within.

Poppy. As a flower of rejuvenation, the poppy was part of Egyptian funerary rites; for the Greeks, it was an emblem both of fertility, left at the shrines of Demeter and Artemis, and of death, for the poppy was said to have grown up in the footsteps of Demeter as she wandered the earth mourning the death of her daughter Persephone. It is also associated with sleep and forgetting.

Rose. Surely the most meaningful flower in the Western tradition, as the lotus is in the Eastern, the rose, "queen of flowers," as it is often called, has long been prized for its color and scent and the exquisite shape of its bud and petals. An emblem of the soul, of perfection attained, of the heart and love, it is also a symbol of rebirth, both physical and spiritual. Greek myth held that the rose sprang from the blood of Adonis, beloved of the goddess Aphrodite; rosebushes were sacred to her, as well as to Athena, who was said to have been born on Rhodes, the "island of roses." The crone goddess Hecate was often portrayed as wearing a garland of five-leafed roses, symbolizing the beginning of a new cycle of life; at the celebration of the Roman *Rosalia,* dishes heaped with roses were offered to the dead.

The rose also figures in mystical thought as an object of spiritual contemplation. The Virgin Mary is the "Mystical Rose," and the rose windows that were the mystical center of the great medieval cathedrals combine the symbolism of the flower with that of the wheel.

Use the rose on your altar as a living *mandala*—look within its petals to the very heart of things.

Shells

As they have been for millennia, shells are part of many contemporary altars and are chosen for both their beauty and their symbolism. A symbol of the feminine, the shell that emerges from the waters epitomizes the power of life and symbolizes rebirth; in Latin, the word *concha* meant both "bivalve" and "vulva." As early as the Upper Paleolithic, shells—particularly cowries, which resemble the female labia—would be buried with the dead, either simply heaped in piles or strung into elaborate necklaces, bracelets, or hip decorations. Grave goods from the sixth millennium include the spiny oyster shell (*spondylus*) and the tusk shell (*dentalium*), often imported from far-away places, another indication of their value. The life-giving magic of the shell was sufficiently powerful that, in many cultures, both real shells and clay models appear in tombs and near shrines and altars; in ancient Egypt, cowrie shells decorated the sarcophagi of the dead. At the fifth-millennium temples on Malta, bivalves filled with red ocher and clay models of shells were found near the altars. On Minoan Crete, seashells were used for the floors of shrines, while the blowing of the triton was used to summon the Goddess.

In the Americas, too, shells were an important part of ritual. The great god Quetzacoatl, the plumed serpent, was often depicted as emerging from the shell of a gastropod; his palace was built of shells. The great temple at Teotihuacan, like others, was decorated with alternating univalves and bivalves. White shells were holy objects possessed of great powers among the White Mountain Apache and the Eastern Woodlands Midewiwin. Among the Navajo, White Shell Woman is either the younger sibling of Changing Woman, the First Mother who provides all, or an epiphany of her. The white shell is her emblem, as are the dawn and the East.

Many people use shells on their altars to signify water or the oceans. I have collected shells for many years, and they remain endlessly fascinating and beautiful to me. I use them as symbols of the feminine and of the multiplicity of the natural world; each, divinely crafted, is unique. They are perfect natural objects for meditation.

Abalone. The abalone shell, with its iridescent lining, was prized by the Navajo; it was associated with the color yellow and the Black Wind (who lived in a house of abalone), just as turquoise was associated with the sun and the redstone with the Yellow Wind. In ritual, abalone was often used to represent the white shell.

Conch. With its extraordinary spiral and the sound it emits when blown into, it is no wonder that the conch has, in many cultures, attained sacral status. Triton, the sea god of Greek myth, had the head and upper body of a man and the tail of a fish; he carried a conch-shell trumpet. The sound of the conch summoned the Goddess from the peaks in Minoan civilization. In Hinduism, Vishnu holds a conch, symbolic of the ocean, the first breath, and the first sound. The left-handed chank—a rare shell whose whorls go counterclockwise rather than clockwise, or "right"—is used by Hindu priests as a sacral instrument. In China, the conch was the symbol of a prosperous voyage and, in Buddhism, the emblem of the voice of Buddha as well as one of the auspicious signs in the footprints of Buddha. The conch is also used in Buddhist worship.

Hold the conch to your ear, and hear the voice of the waters. Make your own inner silence so that you can hear its song.

Cowrie. The cowrie is primarily a female symbol of fertility and rebirth, although, because it has also been used extensively both as money and decoration, it also signifies wealth and good fortune. Cowries, too, have served as talismans and amulets.

The Romans called the cowie *matriculus,* or "little womb." I use the cowrie as an emblem of the feminine and of mystery, for its center within cannot be seen.

Scallop. Though in Christian symbolism the scallop is an emblem of the pilgrim, in ancient times, this shell was firmly associated with the feminine in general and with Aphrodite in particular. The Greek word for the scallop shell, *kteis,* also meant the female genitals. By the fourth century B.C., according to Anne Baring and Jules Cashford, the scallop had become a symbol of the womb of the sea that gave Aphrodite life.

This exquisite altar, built by Cindy Pavlinac in her garden, would be equally evocative, although certainly different, if it were indoors. Two beautiful goddess statues, created by the English artist Philippa Bowers, face each other; they are seated on an octagonal mirror to reflect *chi,* which has a crystal placed on it to increase energy even more. The two are reflected by a lovely standing mirror, as are the tendrils of ivy that surround them, creating a vision of the fluidity and movement inherent in all life.

Sacred Space and the Everyday

In humanity's spiritual past, the cosmic and the individual were inseparable. The understanding of the sacred landscape and the interconnection of all things within it meant that the life experience of each
individual was defined by the larger cosmic order. The entire visible
universe was a revelation of spiritual principles, embodied in deities
for peoples as various as the ancient Egyptians, the Cretans, the
Greeks, the Japanese, and the Native Americans. Shared public rites
and ceremonies marked the passage of calendrical time—the movement from sowing to summer, from harvest to winter—and served to
underscore humanity's essential connection to the larger cycles of nature, the phases of the moon, and the changes in the sun's course. The
consecration of sacred space—the communal building, spanning generations, of sacred precincts from prehistoric Gozo on Malta and
Stonehenge in England to Chartres Cathedral in France and the pueblos in New Mexico—had the effect of defining daily life within the
larger spiritual pattern of the cosmos as well.

Both sacred space and, sometimes, domestic space were oriented
to reveal the cosmic order. The sacred precinct at New Grange in Ireland was designed so that the rising sun of the winter solstice would
shine in and illuminate its interior space, while Stonehenge had both
solar and lunar orientations. The door of the Navajo hogan always
faced east, the direction of the rising sun. The cathedrals from the
eleventh to the sixteenth centuries were positioned to reflect the pattern of the heavens, for the head of the church was oriented toward

the east, "the part of the sky in which the sun rises at the equinox," according to a thirteenth-century source. Within the Christian scheme, the part of the cathedral facing north, the direction associated with cold and darkness, was often consecrated to the Old Testament, while the south face, warm and bathed with light, was devoted to the New Testament. The western facade of most Gothic cathedrals was usually reserved for a representation of the Last Judgment, where, in Emile Male's words, "the setting sun lights up the great scene of the evening of the world's history." Historically, the process by which this pervading sense of spirit was lost was a complicated one.

For many people, reclaiming part of where they live as sacred space is the first step in recovering a pervading sense of the spirit. Whether you decide to use your altar primarily as a reminder of the role spirit plays in your life, as a place of meditation or prayer, or as the focal point for ritual and ceremony is less important, I think, than the step that creating sacred space represents: your conscious intention to make time for both the needs and the goals of the spirit.

Over one hundred years ago, the British philosopher and minister James Martineau reminded his contemporaries that finding God was not a matter of time or place:

> The universe, open to the eye to-day, looks as it did a thousand years ago. . . . We see what all our fathers saw. And if we cannot find God in your house or mine; upon the roadside or the margin of the sea; in the bursting seed or opening flower; in the day duty or the night musing; in the general laugh and the secret grief; in the procession of life, ever entering afresh, and solemnly passing by and dropping off, I do not think we should discern him any more on the grass of Eden, or beneath the moonlight of Gethsemane.

By creating sacred space, we remind ourselves that the world *is* a place of spirit and revelation.

3

Earth as Sacred Space

In a Different Light

Building altars outdoors brings us back to the very beginning of humanity's rituals and rites, which, in their earliest forms, honored the Earth Mother and the cycles of life. Going outside, we place ourselves back in the sacred groves of our ancestors, whose eyes, attuned to a different understanding of the natural world, could see the mark of the divine everywhere. The natural world *was* sacred space. Bringing our spiritual life out of doors is a humbling experience, too, for it reminds us that each of us is only a very small part of the natural world. Going outside reconnects us to the land we live on at a time when most of us no longer feel the ancient links of sun and growth, earth and harvest, rain and plenty. There is a perspective we gain under the broad expanse of sky and the towering shadows of the trees that is often hard to grasp in our noise-filled everyday lives. At the same time, the small miracles of nature—the trilling of a bird's song, the delicate shadow a leaf casts onto the earth, the bright beauty of a blossom—awaken our senses and our spirits, and are a reminder that the natural world is among the great gifts of the spirit.

Creating altars outdoors permits us to get back in touch with the cycle and beauty of natural light that most of us—spending our days in offices, our nights in apartments and houses—no longer experience on a regular basis. Even a familiar corner of the backyard looks utterly different in the noontime sun than it does at the cusp of twilight or beneath the light of the moon. Different lights permit us to see anew. I live on the East Coast, where the change of seasons affects both how you feel and how you live. Even though my favorite time of year is that moment in springtime when a warm rain shower will suddenly— sometimes in a matter of hours—fulfill the promise of the budding trees and the world around my house literally bursts into green, I also love the way the branches of the trees in winter look against the twilight sky: black, bare, and full of sinuous shape, like arms reaching to the heavens.

There are many ways of creating sacred space out of doors and of celebrating and honoring the sacred in nature. Many people regard their gardens as part of their sacred space, a place where they are put in touch with the energy of growth and where they participate in the miracle of nature. Even the simple act of digging in the earth seems to connect us to the ancient rhythms of nature; the scent, texture, and color of the soil combine to wake us up. The forms of life we discover hidden amid the clods of dirt—the earthworms, beetles, sow bugs, even the unwanted grubs and slugs—are a small epiphany of the unseen web of nature. The miracle of life is celebrated in planting the seed or the gnarled corm and watching it bloom as a feathery cosmos or a stately gladiola, while the wind-sown weeds that crowd our plantings are a lesson in humility. Even the dying off of the garden teaches. Tending a garden, too, forces us to focus and slow down; growth has its own timetable. Gardening makes us mindful of the elements and the power of the sun and the moon and puts us back in touch with the Earth Mother.

My own garden has terra-cotta guardian angels that watch over it and a small statue of the Willendorf Goddess; Julie Middleton's gardens—which she regards as "ongoing altars"—are graced by a statue of the Buddha and a winged angel. "Gardening is holy work," she remarks, " because the entire planet is an altar."

In a small corner of another backyard, a statue of Saint Francis sits alongside a smiling Buddha surrounded by a swath of greenery and flowers, far away from the swing set and sandbox where the owner's children play. There is a small bench here, and, in the early evening hours of summer, when the children have gone to bed, it is a place where a mother of three can carve out a small piece of time to think and meditate. Marilyn Goldman has a permanent altar—green and weathered, paled by the sunlight and soaked by the rains—hung in her garden on the post of the arbor. Marilyn leaves small natural offerings in it—a rose, a feather, a rock, a leaf—for the gesture, she says, is "an acknowledgment of nature." From time to time, her young daughter will gift the altar as well.

Though the environmental crisis of the planet, spawned by human neglect and abuse, has, ironically, helped many people focus on the reverence due nature, the idea of looking outside to find the spirit within is very old. On ancient Crete and before, the tree in the sacred grove did not *represent* the goddess; it *was* the goddess, indistinguishable from her. So, for the Greeks, as Vincent Scully has shown in his masterful book *The Earth, the Temple, and the Gods,* the landscape testified to a deity's palpable presence. Befitting an earth goddess, Hera's sacred sites celebrate "the majesty of the surface of the earth," while Demeter's sacred landscapes "evoke its interior, life-giving, death-bringing forces." Not surprisingly, the holy places dedicated to Artemis, goddess of the wilderness, were located in the wild places of Greece—on precipitous cliffs above the shoreline, on verdant crags and crevices in the mountains, and in swamps. This understanding of the varied nature of the landscape, honoring it in all of its aspects, that predates the Greeks by many thousands of years, contains an important lesson in the understanding of natural sacred space.

Whether you are building a temporary altar in a public park or a more permanent one in your own backyard, begin by really looking at your surroundings. What does the natural landscape say to you? What is its spirit? Areas near and around trees bring our focus up from the earth toward the sky, while a site full of scrub and bushes keeps us earthbound. Is the land hilly or flat, curved or linear? Look at the place you intend to build your altar and pay attention to the wind and the sun: is there movement and light? Does the landscape make you more aware? Listen to the place: is it filled with natural sounds—bird calls, rustling, chirping—or is it still? If you are building an altar on your own property, look and listen at different times of the day and night to heighten your awareness of the sacred space.

To see the world in a grain of sand
And heaven in a wildflower,
Hold infinity in the palm of your hand
And eternity in an hour.

WILLIAM BLAKE

Understanding the natural world as the handiwork of the divine or an epiphany of sacred spirit is common to many cultures, a starting point for prayer and meditation. Remember that finding the sacred outdoors need not depend on the grandiose; if you are listening, the inner voice of a beautiful pebble can whisper the glory of the natural world as easily as the Grand Canyon. An altar can just as easily be a small, flat stone with a single flower placed upon it or a gemstone laid on the grass as an elaborately wrought creation.

As you think about the sacred space outside, I offer you a simple story. Lily, the small daughter of a friend, was thrilled by the unseasonable warmth of a sunny winter's day and the green shoots of the early spring bulbs. She wrote a note to the Earth in her five-year-old's wobbly hand. All in capitals, it read, "I LOVE YOU." She dug a tiny hole in the ground, folded the note into it, and covered the note with dirt. Sometime later, she came back to the spot and put a rock on top so that, she explained, "the letter would be safe." *That*, I told her mother later, is an altar.

Sacred Stones

The earliest altar was probably a natural rock or stone set on a holy place, and, in that tradition, perhaps the simplest of all outdoor altars is the cairn, a pile of pebbles or rocks, which has served to mark sacred places, including places of burial, since prehistoric times. In mountainous regions from Europe to the Himalayas, cairns were placed at the top of passes, and travelers would leave offerings. These cairns served both as signs and as thanks for safe passage. The *Hermae* of ancient Greece—quadrangular pillars surmounted by a head or bust, dedicated to Hermes and other deities—that were found on street corners, in front of gates and in the courtyards of homes, before temples and on roads, began as heaps of small stones. The passerby would add a stone or anoint the pile, representing the god, with oil; small offerings, such as fruit or dried figs, were left there as well, sometimes to be shared by the next passerby. Over time, these small heaps of stone were given more formal shape as pillars and were transformed into ubiquitous monuments of everyday devotion.

Piles of stone were built at crossroads in many cultures, for the crossroads is a place traditionally associated with revelation and spirits, sometimes malevolent ones. Symbolically, the crossroads represents choice and, in many places in the world, it was graced with cairns, inscriptions, altars, and shrines, both to propitiate the spirit and to calm the soul of the traveler. In ancient Greece, the crossroads was a place both of the spirits and of the intersection of the known and the unknown, at once the world of the living and the world of the dead. Thus the crossroads was sacred both to Hecate, the triple Goddess, and to Hermes, messenger of the gods, both of whom were honored there with cairns and offerings. Though Hermes was the god of the literal road—the god of signposts—he was also the god of the spiritual path, a mediator between the realms of the spirit, and a god of sleep and dreams.

You can build a cairn in the corner of your garden, under a tree, or, more traditionally, near a gate or threshold. It can be any size, but care will have to be taken with choosing the stones or rocks so that the cairn stays steady. There is something compelling about the simplicity of the cairn and its roots deep in human history, perhaps best illustrated by a story told to me by Sarah Teofanov. It reflects on the fact that while many things change over time, some aspects of how human beings interact do not; the story reminds us, too, that the old ways of doing things may still lie dormant within each of us, half-remembered.

Each day, one of the students in Sarah's altar-building class, a woman in a suburban community, would add to the rough-hewn altar she was making out of found stones and other natural objects at the edge of her property. One morning, she approached the cairn and realized immediately that other stones had been added, and the overall shape reformed. Leaving the anonymously donated stones in place, she continued to build. Day after day, she—and the mysterious other person or persons—continued to work on the cairn until each of them independently decided it was finished. She never met the other altar builder, who remained anonymous, an echo of a time when, two thousand years ago, the lives of two travelers would sometimes intersect—without recognition and only for a brief moment—at a place marked by a heap of stones.

Stones can be used in other ways to demarcate sacred space out of doors. From ancient times, positioning stones or rocks in a circular form has evoked the sacred, perhaps as a visual representation of ancient ritual dances, associated with lunar and solar rites as well as water. In folklore, circles of flat stones found in fields have long been considered places of fairy magic and places of protection. The Native American traditions, too, incorporate the power of the stone circle, for it was the first depiction, among many tribes, of the sacred medicine wheel.

The circle is the great symbol of unity, of closure, and of the cosmos (for more about circles, see page 63); thus it can be used to focus sacred energy outdoors. One woman I know built a circular altar—some four feet in diameter—out of special rocks and stones she had collected on her travels. Each of these rocks—some flat, others irregularly shaped, some worn smooth by water and others pitted—had a specific resonance that connected to places of spiritual importance to her. She worked the earth within the circle and sowed wildflower seeds. Each summer, some of the flowers reseed themselves naturally, and others disappear. She replants the altar, thus participating in the cycle of renewal. For her, this garden altar symbolizes the places she has been and those she has yet to experience.

You can also use stones and rocks to create altars out of sacred symbols: put a circle or triangle of stones outdoors as a way of focusing on the energy of the earth, for example. If you plan on making a place of meditation in your garden, consider putting down a small pathway of stones that lead there, no matter how short or narrow a path it is. You can walk that path slowly as a way of clearing your mind of extraneous thoughts, moving from one plane of life to another. Upright stones, traditional epiphanies of the Goddess in many of her aspects (as the Cretan Britomartis, the Greek Artemis, the Irish Brigit, and the Baltic Laimia) can also be used to focus sacred space out of doors. When you place them, though, be sure that a sizable portion of the rock is buried underground so that it has little likelihood of tipping.

Working with stones and rocks can be immensely pleasurable; I like the feeling and weight of the stone in my hand as well as the way some rocks change color in the light.

The Labyrinth: A Spiritual Path

The rediscovery of the labyrinth as a meditative tool, an outgrowth of the pioneering work of Dr. Lauren Artress at Grace Cathedral in San Francisco and the other labyrinths designed and built in churches and communities all over the United States, has inspired numbers of people to construct labyrinths as part of their sacred space outdoors. For detailed information on the labyrinth, see Dr. Artress's book *Walking a Sacred Path*, listed in Resources and Bibliography.

The labyrinth has an ancient sacral history, going back to ancient Crete and perhaps before, although not as a meditative tool. The earliest human "cathedrals"—the sacred caves of the Paleolithic—were natural labyrinths, and certainly the rites conducted in them, a journey from light into darkness, from the surface of the earth into the center of the earth's body, had both literal and symbolic effect. It seems highly possible that this journey into the labyrinth involved both a symbolic descent, or "death," or journey into mystery, and, at the end, a "rebirth," or return to life on the earth's surface. Our word *labyrinth* means "house of the *labrys*," the ritual double ax of Minoan civilization. Both the ruins at Knossos and the surviving Greek legend of the Minotaur trapped in the labyrinth attest to its importance.

As reconstructed by Vincent Scully, the ritual procession through the manmade labyrinth of Knossos was a symbolic one that echoed the natural forms outside and signified the Goddess's presence. It took its participants from light into darkness and down stairs and then culminated in the low, dark innermost shrine of the Double Axes, a small, cavelike room only twenty-five feet square with an altar and ceremonial objects. Finally, the procession was led back toward the light, back up through the palace complex, through columned courtyards, and finally to the open courts, where the horned mountain and the valley of the Goddess were visible once again.

The ceremonial Cretan labyrinth, usually portrayed as a unicursal seven-circuit labyrinth, is distinct from the tradition of the church labyrinth—eleven concentric circles with the center as the twelfth—that is the model for the one at Grace Cathedral. Often set in stone, as it is at Chartres Cathedral, the church labyrinth is possessed of meaningful symbolism. Both, however, are spiritual paths of revelation. In Dr. Artress's words, "The unicursal path of the labyrinth is what differentiates it and sets it apart as a spiritual tool. The labyrinth does not engage our thinking minds. It invites our intuitive, pattern-seeking mind to come forth."

Either tradition can, of course, be drawn on. Labyrinths can be created in many different ways, some more permanent and time-consuming than others. You can use flour or grain to create the pattern or even nontoxic, earth-friendly spray paint that will dissolve at the first rain. (Cindy Pavlinac points out that anyone who tries to construct a labyrinth out of birdseed only does it once!) More ambitiously, you can build a labyrinth of bricks, either by laying the bricks flat (so that they are the path itself) or by putting them on edge (so that the tamped-down grass between the bricks becomes the path).

If you have an abundance of physical space, time, and energy and want a permanent labyrinth, you can build an earthworks labyrinth, with the form of the maze rising two or three feet high. It can be seeded, planted, or left to catch plants sown by the wind.

Much more ephemeral but no less spiritually rewarding is building a labyrinth at low tide on the beach. This is best done with a group of people, and here the "building" is accomplished by nothing more complicated than walking in the labyrinthine pattern and creating the path with your feet. The labyrinth is, of course, reabsorbed into the waters when you leave.

Cindy built a labyrinth, a spiritual path along which to meditate, out of stones on her deck in a simple, double spiral shape. The stones had been collected by a friend as he traveled the country, so they were evocative of the different parts of North America, including the Southwest and Mexico. Their different colors, shapes, and textures caught the eye: some were volcanic in origin, while others, marked by bits of quartz, glittered in the sun. Cindy would walk this contemplative path in the early morning, when the sun shone on the deck, as a way of getting into the day from the sleep world of the night. Once again, size and scale are less important than intention.

..........,....................

Stones of Reflection: The Zen Garden

Rocks play an extremely important role in the creation of a very different kind of sacred space that is Oriental in its origins, and that can be drawn on in large outdoor spaces or in very small ones: the Zen garden. These dry landscape gardens, created as microcosms of the universe, are actually places of contemplation and meditation, and they work on the natural, symbolic, and metaphysical levels. The Zen garden, which reached its highest point of expression in Japan, was highly influenced by the ancient religion of Shintoism, which venerated both nature spirits and ancestors.

In the Shinto tradition, specific rocks were seen as the abodes of the gods, and their sanctity was made clear by specially woven ropes tied around them, designating a sacred precinct. That legacy plays a part in the creation of a Zen garden in which specifically chosen rocks, raked and patterned sand or gravel, and a bare minimum of plantings (or none at all) offer a stylized vision of the natural world meant for contemplation of humanity's relationship to the cosmos.

Because a Zen garden is meant to be viewed, not walked in, the tiniest of outdoor spaces will, if necessary, suffice for your contemplative garden. Following the Japanese tradition in which the garden was visible from within the domestic quarters or from the temple precinct, you may want to choose a location that permits you to be comfortable while you meditate. For step-by-step directions on creating the garden, please consult Resources.

After you have chosen where to build your Zen garden, the next step is choosing rocks for it. Scale—depending on the size of your garden—is obviously one consideration, but you may also want to follow the Japanese tradition that prefers weathered and uncut stones, stones that either embody the force of the elements or articulate some characteristic of the natural landscape from which they were taken. Thus, rocks smoothed by water or left cragged by wind and erosion are prized, as are those that have rust or growths of moss. Traditionally, round, white, even, or square rocks are not used in a Zen garden.

Groupings of stones in the Zen garden reflect either Buddhist cosmology or events in the Buddha's life or use the symbolism inherent in the shapes of the stones themselves, relating to their use, cultural values, or relationship to landscape. Tradition identifies five shapes of rock: tall vertical, low vertical, reclining, flat, and arching. Zen garden design tends to use rocks in groups of odd numbers, most importantly in threes, reflecting either Heaven, Earth, and Man (a horizontal, a diagonal, a vertical rock posed together) or the Buddhist trinity. The raked gravel or sand in the Zen garden symbolizes water and can be patterned to reflect stillness or movement or to imitate the ever-widening ripple. Maintaining the garden—reconstituting the patterns and keeping the gravel free of debris—is part of the discipline of the garden itself.

Designing the Zen garden is itself an act of spirit, because finding the right balance among the elements requires both an inner and an outer eye. Perhaps what to Western eyes, at least, lends such power to the Zen garden is its *appearance* of simplicity—the austerity of the gravel, the bareness of the rock, the coolness of its colors—and the extraordinary depth of its meaning when, in the process of reflection and quiet, distractions fall away and the spirit is revealed.

Earthworks Altar

You can also create an altar out of the earth itself, and take part, on a miniature scale, in an ancient tradition that involved transforming the very surface of the earth and creating raised surfaces and shapes for religious and ceremonial purposes. Tumuli and mounds were built on both the European and the North American continents not simply to honor the dead (although some were clearly burial places) but also as sacred places of rite. Silbury Hill in England, the largest such mound in Europe, is part of the sacred precinct of Avebury and its standing circular stones. Constructed in the third millennium B.C.E. of successive layers of flint and clay covered with topsoil, this breast-shaped hill is a symbol of the Earth Goddess. In the absence of written records, we don't know why Silbury Hill was built and thousands upon thousands of hours expended, but we do know that it must have been a potent manifestation of the power of the Goddess: even though it was built, layer by layer, basket by basket, by human hands, it flowered and gave birth to new vegetation. The flattened top of the hill suggests that it may well have been an altar, perhaps used for firstfruits or harvest ceremonies.

On the North American continent, the extraordinary peoples now referred to as the Mound Builders, the ancestors of the Native American peoples, built mounds from the Great Lakes to the Gulf of Mexico, from the Mississippi River to the Appalachian Mountains. Though some of the mounds clearly were meant to honor the dead, others—

some built as pyramids, others as cones or elongated slabs, and still others carefully sculpted in the shapes of huge animals—were not. Among the most extraordinary of these are the serpent, winding its way toward a giant egg, that rises up out of a hill in Chillicothe, Ohio, or the thirteen Marching Bears in Iowa. Once again, the intention of the builders is lost to us, although the mounds still inspire awe. Were they oriented toward the stars or sun? Were they built to honor the power of the totem animals or bring that power back to the land? Was building an act of propitiation, or a summons to the spirits? We can only wonder.

An earthworks altar can be formed in any scale that feels comfortable and in any shape you wish; take pleasure in the way the dirt feels between your fingers. You can plant it with seeds or seedling plants, or simply leave it bare. Nature being what it is, the altar won't stay bare for long.

A Spiritual Oasis: The Water Garden

Perhaps nothing is really as soothing to the spirit or as indicative of the holiness of nature as water—its movement, its reflectiveness, its symbolic and literal properties. Water and life-energy are inseparable, and creating a water garden—even a tiny one in a container—can yield a sacred space at once quiet and full of creative energy.

Water gardens surrounded by sacred shade trees with lotuses floating on the surface of the water have a history reaching back to ancient Egypt, where such gardens were built near sacred precincts and temples as well as in domestic space. Once the province only of those lucky enough to have sufficient land and money and a source of flowing water, now—thanks to some thoroughly modern inventions (and a strong back, if you are planning on a pool)—the water garden can be part of just about everyone's sacred space.

Working on a very small scale, a water garden can be set up in a container—essentially any container that can hold water, although if you decide on a half-barrel, you will want to line it with durable plastic so that the materials used to treat the wood (often toxic) do not leach into the water. See Resources for books on how to plant a water garden, either in the ground or in a container.

The most sacred of flowers, the lotus, can be planted in a small water garden as well as a large one, providing a living mandala for the beholder.

....

Garden Altars

The touching of the earth is an act divine—Greetings,
The touching of the earth is an act divine—Greetings,
The touching of the earth is an act divine—Greetings,
I have come—Greetings,
The touching of the earth is an act divine—Greetings.

The digging into the earth is an act divine—Greetings,
The digging into the earth is an act divine—Greetings,
The digging into the earth is an act divine—Greetings,
I have come—Greetings,
The digging into the earth is an act divine—Greetings.

OSAGE, "SONG OF THE VIGIL"

Understanding your garden as a sacred space helps focus both intentions and thoughts. Creating a living altar to Mother Earth, one that attracts birds and butterflies and other living creatures to your sacred space, is simply a matter of choosing the right flowers and plants to attract them. Remember as you begin work that birds will need both cover and places to perch, in the form of trees and shrubs such as dogwood, elm, birch, juniper, and creeping myrtle. If there are few trees, you might try to keep a corner of the garden wild and overgrown to fill the need for cover and to attract insects for the birds to eat. Plant sunflowers, painted calliopsis, coreopsis, cosmos, and millet for seed, while the berries of vines such as Virginia creeper and bittersweet will attract many varieties of birds. The berries of certain shrubs, euonymus and burning bush among them, will also bring these guardians of the spirit to your yard. Hummingbirds—those delicate sylphs of the air—are attracted to red, tubular flowers such as trumpet creeper but also feed on columbine, zinnia, sweet william, and honeysuckle. Remember, too, to provide the birds with a source of water.

Each summer, all manner of butterflies—the showy monarchs and swallowtails, the painted ladies, and the ubiquitous cabbage whites— feed upon the flowers in my garden, feasting, along with the bees, on the sweetness of the hydrangeas. They light on the gloriosa daisies and the different kinds of salvia I have planted. My daughter and I take great pleasure in these glorious creatures who bridge the gap between earth and sky with delicate flight, and, once you have watched them closely and carefully, it is no surprise that they were once seen as epiphanies of the Earth Mother. To attract butterflies to your living altar, you might plant purple cone flowers, buddleia, daisies, lobelia, nicotiana, salvia, lupine, globe amaranth, and tithonia, among other flowers. If you have a birdbath, put a stone or two in it for the butterflies, since they need to light just above the waterline to sip.

Remember, as you create your altar garden, to keep the scale manageable so that you have the time not only to participate in its upkeep but also to benefit from the haven it offers.

The sacred space of the garden can be worked to encompass a symbolic dimension that articulates—in the forms of the plantings themselves, their combination, or their colors—a spiritual concept, hopes or aspirations, or even a stage of life.

Ed, who only recently moved to the West Coast from the East where he was born and raised and has lived most of his adult life, has created a garden of transition, honoring and giving voice to the change in his life. It is a place where he will burn candles, bring his bowls and other sacred objects, perform dedications, or simply think.

The garden itself is planted on a two-foot-high terrace—which makes it literally altar-shaped—against an eastern wall covered in vines. He chose this place on the property deliberately because of its eastern orientation, which for him symbolizes both the place of the rising sun, the future, and his own place of origin and roots. As a recently transplanted easterner, he still associates that direction with the ocean and the beach, a landscape that has played an important role in his life. The terrace had a tree rose planted long ago that, for Ed, has strong associations with family. All her life, his late grandmother planted and tended exquisite rosebushes, which bloomed in profusion in her modest but wonderfully tended backyard. The site was also perfect for his garden of transition since it is the first thing he sees when he leaves the house; in addition, all visitors to his home must pass it on the way in.

Ed planted the garden with deliberately contrasting plants—tall verticals set against delicate, low-growing plants—to symbolize the *yin* and *yang* nature of transition and change. Sansevieria and gladiola tower in the back, while exquisite johnny-jump-ups and pansies grow in the front. While he weeds, he has been careful not to pull two "mystery" plants, neither of which he put in the garden and both of which survived his clearing of the garden space. For him, they represent the unknown, which is always part of any transition.

Three found objects complete the altar garden of transition: a figurine of a goddess in a Madonna-like stance with a hollowed belly where a candle can be placed; a large stone, which might be fashioned or could equally be natural, which has a hollowed center and a second stone—with a phalluslike shape—placed within it, like a mortar and pestle; and a hand-painted, platelike peace symbol, which looks for all the world as if it was painted by a child long ago. Ed does not know the provenance of any of these objects, or how they were once used; they too are establishing a new identity in his garden of transition.

The leaf becomes flower when it loves.
The flower becomes fruit when it worships.
RABINDRANATH TAGORE

An entire garden can become sacred space in other ways as well. To honor and integrate the changes in her body and life, Nancy Blair has created a crone's garden dedicated to Hecate, the triple goddess of the three stages of a woman's life—maiden, matron, crone. At the center of it is an altar. The garden was dedicated in a ceremony under the full moon to pull energy up from the ground and down from Hecate. From the roughly three-foot circle in the center radiate three-foot-wide paths—the traditional *tri via,* or crossroads, sacred to Hecate—paved with white gravel that lead to other places in the yard. The lush garden (it benefits from a Mediterranean climate) has grown up around the paths—planted with red flowers such as hibiscus, symbolic of the blood-force of the goddess, white periwinkles, and sunflowers as well as cruciferous vegetables. There is an herb garden as well, with vitex, tarragon, borage, oregano, thyme, bee balm, and scented geraniums, creating a haven for butterflies and other wildlife. Another area of the garden is devoted to native plants, inviting them into the circle that is the garden.

At the very center is the altar dedicated to the beginning of the crone stage of Nancy's life—the traditional time of wisdom and understanding, when a woman's full powers are no longer distracted by the pulls of the menstrual cycles. On a pink marble slab some two feet wide stand two statues drawn from ancient models but sculpted by Nancy: a kneeling winged Isis—magisterial, with the horned solar disk on her head—and a Hecate, Queen of the Crones, shown in her triple aspect. Sacred snakes, full of energy, coil around her, while Hecate herself holds torches in each hand. She is crowned with ears of grain. A small representation of an owl is on the altar, as well as beautifully shaped and whorled stones and rocks. Nancy will gift the altar with candles, as well as cut gladiolas and gladiola corms, symbolic of the cycle of life beginning once again.

Off one of the paths leading to the altar is a large area of aloe, the healing plant, and within it is a small sanctuary or altar devoted to Inanna, the great goddess of the Sumerians, Queen of Heaven and Earth. This small area has been created as a point of meditation, a stopping place on the path that leads to the altar itself.

The altar and the sacred garden are a place for Nancy to honor her bleeding times and the cycles and rhythms of her body, her life, and the greater cycle of nature that they are a part of. Prayers and rituals performed here remind Nancy to, in her words, "claim my power and soar!"

Using sacred imagery outdoors or in the garden, regardless of the tradition from which it is drawn, is another way of affirming the spiritual nature of the world. Nestled among the plants in Nancy Blair's garden, with rocks and a crystal by her side, is a small statue of the goddess Inanna, a visual reminder of the strong ties between the feminine and nature. As Nancy says, "Inanna reminds me to nurture *myself* during my journey."

Tree Altars

Ironically, *not* seeing trees as sacred or possessed of spirit is a comparatively recent development in human history. For millennia, trees were the first altars, as well as guardians. Symbols of the life force that reached from their roots in the underworld up through the dome of the sky, trees were inseparable from the divine. In many cultures, including the Native American, trees were the portal to higher understanding. (For more about trees, see page 147.) Today, as people strive to get back in touch with ancient understandings that can ameliorate the condition of both the planet and its denizens, honoring the trees around us seems a necessary and important step.

Observation only deepens our respect for the natural world. Identify your tree, if you can, and watch it change over the seasons, for even an evergreen will change over the course of a year. Try to visualize the extraordinary energy, invisible to our eyes, that rises from its roots to its top. If it is a tree you are responsible for, on your own property, take care of it, making sure it stays healthy. Honor the tree as a vital link in the beauty that surrounds you.

Altars dedicated to trees can take the form of simple offerings—a prayer or crystal, a stone or a flower—or can be made more elaborate. Some people hang ornaments or prayer flags on their trees, while others prefer to let the natural beauty of the living being speak for itself. As you decide on the form you want your altar to take, you may want to remember this exquisite Chinook blessing:

May all I say and all I think
be in harmony with thee,
God within me, God beyond me,
maker of the trees.

In me be the windswept truth of shorepine,
fragrance of balsam and spruce,
the grace of hemlock.
In me the truth of douglas fir, straight, tall,
strong-trunked land hero of fireproof bark.
Sheltering tree of life, cedar's truth be mine,
cypress truth, juniper aroma, strength of yew.

May all I say and all I think
be in harmony with thee,
God within me, God beyond me,
maker of the trees.
In me be the truth of stream-lover willow
soil-giving alder
hazel of sweet nuts, wisdom-branching oak.

In me the joy of crabapple, greatmaple, vinemaple,
cleansing cascara and lovely dogwood.
Amid the gracious truth of the copper branched arbutus
bright with colour and fragrance,
be with me on the Earth.

May all I say and all I think
be in harmony with thee,
God within me, God beyond me,
maker of the trees.

Outside Altars for Special Occasions

The traditional calendar of earth-honoring ceremonies—the summer and winter solstices, the March and September equinoxes, as well as the festivals that mark the quarter points in-between—were conducted out of doors, and many people, following the old traditions, have continued the practice, building altars outside if weather permits. Each of these celebrations requires a slightly different altar-building vocabulary, which you may vary according to your own vision.

The equinox—the twice-yearly moment when day and night are precisely the same length—is, as Cindy points out, a time of balance, and thus she builds her altars to reflect the moment, choosing pairs of objects, often opposites: light and dark, dry and wet, heavy and light. The solstices, which she regards as more extreme moments in the year, are celebrated both indoors and out, usually with fire, as is traditional. She honors these moments of transformation by aligning her altars with the sunrise so as to catch the first ray of light upon them, an act that reaches far back in time to sacred places such as New Grange in Ireland, and by burning written prayers or intentions left on the altar in the previous months to signify transformation. Celebrating the winter solstice indoors near the fireplace in her group rituals, Ann Evans also uses the powerful symbolism of fire. The winter solstice is, as she says, a time associated with "darkness, rest, storytelling, quiet, and contemplation." It is also a moment to honor "what has ended and must be released." Thus, the ritual includes the burning of ten things "we are willing to release, either because they have served their purpose or because they are holding us back." The act of release is balanced by a calling forth of things the participants are willing to bring into their lives.

Building altars for the celebration of a specific moment implies impermanence, unlike the permanence of the domestic altar, which can stay in the same form for months. There is a lesson in impermanence itself, as witnessed by the story told to me by Cindy about a group altar she helped build to celebrate Beltane, the traditional Celtic May Day, which begins at the moonrise of the previous evening. Beltane was a festival to increase the fertility of all things—in the fields and in the home—and was a symbolic bringing in of new life. Traditionally, bonfires, symbolic of the life force of the sun, as well as maypole dances were part of Beltane's rituals. This contemporary celebration took place on a beach with a simple altar built onto the sand out of a frame constructed of driftwood. The altar was gifted with things found on the beach itself—rocks and pebbles, bits of wood and shell—as well as objects the participants had brought, including a mirror, a statue of an African goddess, and flowers. Rose petals, which Cindy had collected from one of her own bushes, were scattered over and around the altar. The rituals included feasting, drumming, and dancing, with the participants leaping over the bonfire as people did many centuries ago. Later, the celebrants danced around a newly made maypole and, with ceremony, burned the maypole from the year before.

A second altar was built at low tide, this one specifically meant to be returned to the life-giving ocean. Shaped like a world mountain of sand, it was made up of natural things—bits of kelp and seaweed, stones, and driftwood—all of which were meant to be swept into the ocean at the full tide as a gift. Prayers and blessings were said silently or with voice into the wind, and then the participants turned their back on the altar, giving it back to the mighty waters.

A song of the rolling earth, and of words according,
Were you thinking that those were the words, those upright
    lines?
those curves, angles, dots?
No, those are not the words, the substantial words are in the
    ground and sea,
They are in the air, they are in you.

WALT WHITMAN

Building altars outside permits us to celebrate and honor our connection to the blue planet we share with other forms of life, some a part of our daily lives and others invisible to our eyes but not to our spirits. Building an altar takes the words that are in us and gives them a physical form—an act of articulation that brings thoughts and feelings into a different form of reality—and permits us to truly hear them.

Altars and Transformation

Creating sacred space is a process. The act of building an altar changes us and our sense of ourselves in time and space, and that, in turn, changes the next sacred space we choose to create. Because altar building is a physical activity, it takes what we know emotionally and intellectually—learned from life experience and other people, words and books—and transforms it into a different kind of knowledge and seeing. Each successive altar we build is connected both to the last and to the next, and to the stages in our own spiritual development those sacred spaces represent.

Building altars permits us to avail ourselves of the affirming and empowering aspects of change. Human life is full of changes that are, in many important ways, beyond our control, and the most profound are the most difficult. The things that matter to us most—existence itself, love and intimacy, health and well-being, and happiness—are all subject to the larger cycles of life and death, attainment and loss. Change, of necessity, always involves both a step forward *and* a step back, a letting go *and* a reaching out. Creating sacred space helps us come to terms with change in all of its aspects and allows us to focus on the energy of change in positive ways.

One of the most ancient symbols of change and transformation known to humanity is the snake. Serpentine designs were incised on sacred places thousands and thousands of years ago to capture the energy and transformative power of the snake, who sheds its skin only to grow a new one; real snakes, too, were kept in homes as well as in sanctified places to imbue a physical location with their powers of transformation. This year, I got firsthand knowledge of the snake when my daughter, a budding herpetologist, acquired one that has grown steadily from a small hatchling to an almost adolescent. To my surprise, though, the snake's shedding is itself not without discomfort; skin does not, as the symbolism might have you believe, fall effortlessly from the snake's body. Both in the wild and in captivity, the snake has to work to get the shed off—squeezing itself through small places or up against bushes or rough branches—to facilitate the process.

Not even the snake transforms itself without the meaningful effort we call work.

In that sense, creating sacred space is "work." The energy and thoughtfulness you put into creating sacred space in your home, your office, or your garden in turn creates new energy and thoughtfulness. Sacred space can become a starting place for new journeys, new thoughts, and new efforts.

Like any other process, the creation of sacred space and the spirit takes place over time. Remember, as you work and build, the words of Saint Francis de Sales, who well understood the transformation of the spirit through meditation: "Be patient till your wings are grown."

Resources

Following are retail and mail order sources for both altar materials and further reading organized by section and subsection, where applicable. Many of the resources carry a variety of altar-related items, so please skim all the entries. A starred entry (*) indicates either a source with which I am personally familiar or a book that I consider especially helpful. For full publishing information, please see the bibliography.

The Language of Sacred Space

Suggested Reading

*Vincent Scully, *The Earth, the Temple, and the Gods*

Consultation Services

Oralee Stiles, Spiritual Director, 2909 Northeast 32nd Avenue, Portland, OR 97212; (503) 288–8058. Oralee teaches how to build altars and create sacred space.

Deciding Placement

Suggested Reading

On *feng shui:*

*William Spear, *Feng Shui Made Easy*

Karen Kingston, *Creating Sacred Space with Feng Shui*

Kristen Lagatree, *Feng Shui*

On Native American traditions:

*Brooke Medicine Eagle, *Buffalo Woman Comes Singing*

Resources

Feng Shui Warehouse, P.O. Box 6689, San Diego, CA 92166; (800) 399–1599; fax (800) 997–9831. Crystals, flutes, octagonal mirrors, wind chimes, fountains, and more, plus many books on the subject, are available from this catalogue source.

Choosing Materials

*Inexpensive unfinished niche altars, which you can paint, stain, or decorate youself (pictured on page 159), are available from Sidedoor Press, 2934 Lomita Road, Santa Barbara, CA 93105; (805) 563–2279.

For Buddhist altar shelves and cabinets: Shasta Abbey Buddhist Supplies, P.O. Box 199, Mt. Shasta, CA 96067; (800) 653–3315. In addition, they carry statuary, incense burners, gongs, and other ritual items.

Handcrafted altars (10⅜ high, 16⅞ by 27¼ wide) in aromatic cedarwood, naturally finished and without metal fittings, are available from Barabra Steele, P.O. Box 2424, Guerneville, CA 95446–2424; (510) 848–1042. Barbara will also make custom altars.

Three Jewels Design, P.O. Box 151116, San Rafael, CA 94915; (415) 258–9359. Traditional Japanese tools and a design based on Tibetan architecture distinguish these hand-crafted and made-to-order wooden shrines. Designed for both the home and travel (they fold out), they are created and designed by Sherry Freeman in your choice of three woods from nonendangered species.

Cloth

Suggested Reading

Elizabeth Wayland Barber, *Women's Work*

Resources

Gifts of the Spirit, P.O. Box 772, Belle Meade, NJ 08502, carries batik altar cloths, as well as candles and incense and hand-crafted *malas* and rosaries.

Statuary

Suggested Reading

Joseph Campbell, *The Mythic Image*

Marija Gimbutas, *The Language of the Goddess*

Merlin Stone, *When God Was a Woman*

Resources

*The Great Goddess Collection™, Star River Productions, Inc., P.O. Box 510642, Melbourne Beach, FL 32951; (407) 953–8085; fax (407) 953–8202. Exquisitely modeled images of the divine feminine created by artist Nancy Blair at fair prices with full satisfaction guaranteed.

JBL Statues, P.O. Box 163, Crozet, VA 22932. This company charges $2.00 for its catalogue and has a wide range of statues from many cultures.

DharmaCrafts, 405 Waltham Street, Suite 234, Lexington, MA 02173. A catalogue of Buddhist meditation supplies, including incense, bells, and gongs, it also features statuary.

Home of the Buddhas, 1223 Summerwind Way, Milpitas, CA 95035; (800) 592–8332; fax (408) 262–9114. Statues of Buddha, Ganesha, Tara, among others.

Cindy Pavlinac, Sacred Land Photography, P.O. Box 613, Mill Valley, CA 94942. Beautiful original photographs of sacred places, including Ancient Greece and the British Isles, as well as Native American sites.

Altar Ware

Resources

Altar Egos Gallery, 110 West Houston Street, New York, NY 10012; (212) 677–9588. Everything for the altar, from statues, candles, clothes, offering bowls, cauldrons and chalices, ritual oils, and incense.

The Hero's Journey, 2440 Broadway, New York, NY 10024; (212) 874–4630. This retail outlet carries books, pottery, candles, Tibetan artifacts, singing bowls, tonkas, drums, and rattles.

Kindred Spirits, 22 South Fullerton Avenue, Montclair, NJ 07042; (973) 746–5988. This store carries sacred objects and statuary, meditation tools, drums, singing bowls, herbs and incense, chimes, fountains, and books.

The Red Rose Collection, 826 Burlway, Burlingame, CA 94010; (800) 220–ROSE. A general catalogue that often carries altar-related wares, including bowls and smudge pots. Their retail store, in San Francisco, is at 2251 Chestnut Street; (415) 776–6871.

Signs and Symbols

Suggested Reading

Hans Biedermann, *Dictionary of Symbolism*

Jean Chevalier and Alain Gheerbrant, *The Penguin Dictionary of Symbolism*

Barbara Walker, *The Women's Dictionary of Symbols and Sacred Objects*

Energizing Sacred Space

Suggested Reading

*Denise Linn, *Sacred Space*

Resources

Mystic Trader, 1334 Pacific Avenue, Forest Grove, OR 97116; (800) 634–9057. This catalogue offers a potpourri of items, from statuary to musical instruments to stupas to incense and smudge.

Soul Journey, 9 Main Street, Butler, NJ 07405; (973) 838–6564; fax (973) 838–1471. This retail store also has a mail order catalogue featuring a large selection of books as well as runes and other divination tools, crystals, herbs, incense, and smudges.

The Pyramid Collection, Altid Park, P.O. Box 3333, Chelmsford, MA 01824–0933; (800) 333–4220. Another general catalogue with a range of items, including crystals, tapes, and CDs.

The Power of Scent

Resources

The Candle Shop, 118 Christopher Street, New York, NY 10014; (212) 989–0148. A large variety of candles, including those specifically for ritual, both scented and unscented.

Kamala Perfumes, Inc., 627 ½ East Green Street, Champaign, IL 61820; (217) 367–0207. Incense and incense burners, over ninety different kinds of essential oils, as well as candles and lotions; send $1.50 for a catalogue.

MoonScents and Magickal Blends, P.O. Box 180310, Boston, MA 02118–0310; (800) 386–7417; fax (617) 482–0804. In addition to books, gifts, crystals, and paraphernalia for Earth-based rituals, this catalogue carries a large selection of incense, oils, herbal kits, and dried herbs.

Tools for Prayer and Meditation

Suggested Reading

*Margot Astrov, *The Winged Serpent* (a superb anthology of Native American prayers, poems, myths)

*John Bierhorst, *The Sacred Path*

*Nancy Blair, *Goddesses for Every Season*

*Peg Streep, *The Sacred Journey,* illustrated by Claudia Karabaic Sargent

Elizabeth Roberts and Elias Amadon, eds, *Earth Prayers from Around the World*

Consultation Services

Ann Evans, M.Div., A Rite to Remember, 5337 College Avenue, Suite 116, Oakland, CA 94618; (510) 339–7561. Ceremonies and rituals to celebrate life.

Resources

Dharmaware, 54 C Tinker Street, Woodstock, NY 12498; (914) 679–4900. This shop and its catalogue carry high-quality meditation materials, including *malas,* as well as statues, drums, bells and *dorjes,* and sacred art.

Isabella, 2780 Via Orange Way, Suite B, Spring Valley, CA 91978; (619) 670–5200 or (800) 777–5205. A mail order catalogue of books and other spiritual tools, including runes, smudge, candles.

Sounds and Energy

Resources

All One Tribe Drums, P.O. Drawer N, Taos, NM 87571; (800) 442–DRUM. Carries seventeen types of one-sided shaman's drums with either a patented sheepskin-and-leather handle or the traditional rawhide handle. These high-quality drums, hand-crafted by Native Americans, can be purchased unembellished or with specially commissioned, signed artwork in both Native American designs and more general ones, such as eternal spirals.

Bodhisattva Trading Co., Inc., 11301 W. Olympic Blvd., Suite 424, W. Los Angeles, CA 90064; (800) 588–5350. Tibetan singing bowls, *drilbus* and *dorjes,* Tingshaw, as well as CDs and cassettes, are available from this mail order source.

Gemstones, Minerals, and Metals

Suggested Reading

*Barbara Walker, *The Book of Sacred Stones*

Resources

Earth Star Connection®, 1218 31st Street, N.W., Washington, DC 20007; (202) 965–2989. In addition to books, tapes, candles and incense, Zuni fetishes, drums and rattles, this store has a large collection of crystals and minerals, stocking over a hundred types.

Sanctuary, 32 Church Street, Montclair, NJ 07042; (973) 509–7707. This retail store carries crystals, gems, oils, altars, drums, incense, and smudges.

The Nature Company, P.O. Box 188, Florence, KY 41022; call (800) 227–1114 for the mail order catalogue or the location of the nearest retail store. This company carries a large collection of gemstones and minerals, as well as fetishes.

Animals, Totems, and Guardians

Suggested Reading

Hal Zina Bennett, *Zuni Fetishes*

Michael Harner, *The Way of the Shaman*

Buffie Johnson, *Lady of the Beasts*

Jamie Sams and David Carson, *Medicine Cards*

Brad Steiger, *Totems*

The Tree of Life: Boughs and Leaves

Suggested Reading

Robert Graves, *The White Goddess*

Herbs and Spices

Suggested Reading

M. Grieve, *A Modern Herbal*

Resources

Aphrodesia, 264 Bleecker Street, New York, NY 10014;
(212) 989–6460. All varieties of herbs—for culinary, medicinal,
and ritual use—as well as herbs for smudging.

Flowerpower, Inc., 406 East 9th Street, New York, NY 10009;
(212) 982–6664. This retail store carries dried herbs, tinctures,
and oils.

Earth as Sacred Space

Sacred Stones

Suggested Reading

Sibylle von Cles-Redon, *The Realm of the Great Goddess*

The Labryinth: A Spiritual Path

Suggested Reading

Lauren A. Artress, *Walking a Sacred Path*

Stones of Reflection: The Zen Garden

Suggested Reading

Philip Cave, *Creating Japanese Gardens*

David H. Engel, *A Thousand Mountains, a Million Hills*

Teiju Itoh, *Space and Illusion in the Japanese Garden*

The Japanese Garden Society of Oregon with Kate Jerome,
Oriental Gardening

Günter Nitschle, *Japanese Gardens*

Maggie Oster, *Reflections of the Spirit*

Kiyoshi Seike, Masanobyu Kudo, and David H. Engel, *A Japanese Touch for Your Garden*

A Spiritual Oasis: The Water Garden

Suggested Reading

*Joseph Tomocik with Leslie Garisto, *Water Gardening*

Judy Glattstein, *Waterscaping*

D. G. Hessayon, *The Rock and Water Garden Expert*

Anthony Paul and Yvonne Rees, *The Water Garden*

Peter Stadelmann, *Water Gardens*

Resources

The WaterWorks, 111 East Fairmont Street, Coopersburg, PA 18036; (800) 360–LILY. Pumps, fountains, linings, filtration systems, and everything else for a water garden, including water lilies and lotuses.

Lilypons Watergardens, P.O. Box 14, Buckeyestown, MD 21717; (800) 723–7667; or P.O. Box 188, Brookshire, TX 77423; (800) 765–5459; or P.O. Box 1130, Thermal, CA 92274; (800) 365–5459. Complete water garden supplies.

Van Ness Watergardens, 2460 N. Euclid Avenue, Upland, CA 91784; (909) 982–2425. Complete water garden supplies.

Garden Altars

Resources

Sophia Center, P.O. Box 128, Marylhurst, OR 97036; (503) 636–5151. In addition to Hearthstones (stones with affirmations written on them), Blessing Wands, and statues for sacred spaces, this nonprofit organization also sells Earth "seeds"—tiny terracotta "seeds" with images of goddesses, angels, or the Virgin Mary—to "plant" into the Earth as a way of honoring her. I love them!

Bibliography

Armstong, A. H. "The Ancient and Continuing Pieties of the Greek World," in *Classical Mediterranean Spirituality*, edited by A. H. Armstong.

Armstrong, A. H., ed. *Classical Mediterranean Spirituality: Egyptian, Greek, Roman*. New York: The Crossroad Publishing Company, 1986.

Artress, Lauren A. *Walking a Sacred Path: Rediscovering the Labyrinth as a Spiritual Tool*. New York: Riverhead Books, 1995.

Astrov, Margot. *The Winged Serpent: American Indian Prose and Poetry*. Boston: Beacon Press, 1992.

Barber, Elizabeth Wayland. *Women's Work: The First 20,000 Years*. New York: W. W. Norton & Company, 1994.

Baring, Anne, and Jules Cashford. *The Myth of the Goddess: Evolution of an Image*. London: Viking Arkana, 1991.

Bennett, Hal Zina. *Zuni Fetishes: Using Native American Objects for Meditation, Reflection, and Insight*. San Francisco: HarperSanFrancisco, 1993.

Berwick, Ann. *Holistic Aromatherapy: Balance the Body and the Soul with Essential Oils*. St. Paul, MN: Llwellyn Publications, 1994.

Beyer, Stephan. *The Cult of Tara: Magic and Ritual in Tibet*. Berkeley and Los Angeles: University of California Press, 1978.

Biedermann, Hans. *Dictionary of Symbolism*. Translated by James Hulbert. New York: Facts on File, 1992.

Bierhorst, John, ed. *The Sacred Path: Spells, Prayers, and Power Songs of the American Indians*. New York: Quill Books, 1984.

Blair, Nancy. *Goddesses for Every Season*. Rockport, MA: Element Books, 1995.

Bremiss, Leslie. *The Complete Book of Herbs*. New York: Viking Studio Books, 1988.

Budge, E. A. Wallis. *Amulets and Superstitions*. New York: Dover Publications, 1978.

———. *The Gods of the Egyptians*. 2 vols. Reprint. New York: Dover Publications, 1969.

Campbell, Joseph. *The Flight of the Wild Gander*. New York: HarperPerennial, 1990.

———. *The Mythic Image*. Princeton: Princeton University Press, 1974.

Campbell, Joseph, with Bill Moyers. *The Power of Myth*. New York: Doubleday and Company, 1988.

Cave, Philip. *Creating Japanese Gardens*. Rutland, VT: Charles E. Tuttle Company, 1993.

Chevalier, Jean, and Alain Gheerbrant. *The Penguin Dictionary of Symbols*. Translated by John Buchanan-Brown. New York and London: Penguin Books, 1996.

Cirlot, J. E. *A Dictionary of Symbols*. Translated by Jack Sage. New York: Philosophical Library, 1971.

Cunningham, Scott. *Cunningham's Encyclopedia of Crystal, Gem, and Metal Magic*. St. Paul, MN: Llwellyn Publications, 1993.

Dean, Kenneth. *Taoist Ritual and Popular Cults of Southeast China*. Princeton, NJ: Princeton University Press, 1993.

Engel, David H. *A Thousand Mountains, a Million Hills: Creating the Rock Work of Japanese Gardens*. Tokyo: Shufunotomo/Japan Publications, Kodansha America, 1995.

Erman, Adolf. *Life in Ancient Egypt*. Translated by H. M. Tirard. New York: Dover Publications, 1971.

Ferguson, George. *Signs and Symbols in Christian Art*. New York: Oxford University Press, 1971.

Fischer-Schreiber, Ingrid, Franz-Karl Ehrhard, and Michael S. Diener. *The Shambhala Dictionary of Buddhism and Zen*. Boston: Shambhala Publications, 1991.

Gimbutas, Marija. *The Civilization of the Goddess*. San Francisco: HarperSanFrancisco, 1991.

———. *The Goddesses and Gods of Old Europe: Myths and Cult Images*. Berkeley and Los Angeles: University of California Press, 1982.

———. *The Language of the Goddess*. San Francisco: Harper & Row, 1989.

Glattstein, Judy. *Waterscaping: Plants and Ideas for Natural and Created Water Gardens*. Pownal, VT: Storey Communications, 1994.

Goldsmith, Elizabeth. *Ancient Pagan Symbols*. New York: G. P. Putnam's Sons, 1929.

Gordon, Lesley. *Green Magic: Flowers, Plants, and Herbs in Lore and Legend*. New York: Viking Press, 1977.

Graves, Robert. *The Greek Myths*. 2 vols. London: Penguin Books, 1990.

———. *The White Goddess*. Amended and enlarged edition. New York: Farrar, Straus & Giroux, 1978.

Grieve, M. *A Modern Herbal*. 2 vols. New York: Dover Publications, 1971.

Harner, Michael. *The Way of the Shaman: A Guide to Power and Healing*. New York: Bantam Books, 1980.

Harvey, Paul. *The Oxford Companion to Classical Literature*. Oxford: Clarendon Press, 1946.

Hessayon, D. G. *The Rock and Water Garden Expert*. London: Expert Books, 1993.

Huxley, Francis. *The Way of the Sacred*. Garden City, NY: Doubleday and Company, 1974.

Itoh, Teiju. *Space and Illusion in the Japanese Garden*. New York, Tokyo, and Kyoto: Weatherhill/Tonkosha, 1988.

James, E. O. *The Ancient Gods*. New York: G. P. Putnam's Sons, 1960.

———. *From Cave to Cathedral: Temples and Shrines of Prehistoric, Classical, and Early Christian Times*. New York and Washington: Frederick A. Praeger, 1965.

———. *The Cult of the Mother Goddess*. Reprint. New York: Barnes and Noble Books, 1994.

The Japanese Garden Society of Oregon with Kate Jerome, *Oriental Gardening*. New York: Pantheon Books, 1996.

Johnson, Buffie. *Lady of the Beasts: Ancient Images of the Goddess and Her Sacred Animals*. San Francisco: Harper & Row, 1988.

Kingston, Karen. *Creating Sacred Space with Feng Shui: Learn the Art of Space Clearing and Bring New Energy into Your Life*. New York: Broadway Books, 1997.

Kowalchik, Claire, and William H. Hylton, eds. *Rodale's Illustrated Encyclopedia of Herbs*. Emmaus, PA: Rodale Press, 1987.

Kunz, George Fredrick. *The Curious Lore of Precious Stones*. New York: Dover Publications, 1971.

———. *Gems and Precious Stones of North America*. New York: Dover Publications, 1968.

Lagatree, Kristen M. *Feng Shui: Arranging Your Home to Change Your Life*. New York: Villard Books, 1996.

Larrington, Carolyne, ed. *The Feminist Companion to Mythology*. London: Pandora Press, 1992.

Leach, Maria, and Jerome Fried, eds. *Funk and Wagnalls Standard Dictionary of Folklore, Mythology, and Legend*. New York: Harper & Row, 1984.

Linn, Denise. *Sacred Space: Clearing and Enhancing the Energy of Your Home*. New York: Ballantine Books, 1995.

Loewe, Michael, and Carmen Blacker, eds. *Oracles and Divination*. Boulder, CO: Shambala, 1981.

Male, Emile. *The Gothic Image*. New York: Harper & Row Publishers, 1958.

Martin, Laura C. *Garden Flower Folklore*. Chester, CT: The Globe Pequot Press, 1987.

———. *Wildflower Folklore*. Chester, CT: The Globe Pequot Press, 1983.

McGaa, Ed, Eagle Man. *Mother Earth Spirituality: Native American Paths to Healing Ourselves and Our World*. San Francisco: HarperSanFrancisco, 1990.

Medicine Eagle, Brooke. *Buffalo Woman Comes Singing*. New York: Ballantine Books, 1991.

Moore, Albert C. *Iconography of Religions: An Introduction*. Philadelphia: Fortress Press, 1977.

Neumann, Erich. *The Great Mother: An Analysis of the Archetype*. Translated by Ralph Mannheim. Princeton, NJ: Princeton University Press, 1974.

Nitschle, Günter. *Japanese Gardens: Right Angle and Natural Form*. Cologne: Benedikt Taschen Verlag, 1993.

Oster, Maggie. *Reflections of the Spirit: Japanese Gardens in America*. New York: Dutton Studio Books, 1993.

Paul, Anthony, and Yvonne Rees, *The Water Garden*. New York: Penguin Books, 1986.

Reichard, Gladys A. *Navaho Religion: A Study of Symbolism*. Princeton, NJ: Princeton University Press, 1990.

Roberts, Elizabeth, and Elias Amidon, eds. *Earth Prayers from Around the World: 365 Prayers, Poems, and Invocations for Honoring the Earth*. San Francisco: HarperSanFrancisco, 1991.

———. *Life Prayers: 365 Prayers, Blessings, and Affirmations to Celebrate the Human Journey*. San Francisco: HarperSanFrancisco, 1996.

Rohde, Eleanour Sinclair. *The Old English Herbals*. Reprint. New York: Dover Publications, 1971.

Rossbach, Sarah. *Feng Shui: The Chinese Art of Placement*. New York: E. P. Dutton, 1983.

Saffrey, H. D. "The Piety and Prayers of Ordinary Men and Women in Late Antiquity," in *Classical Mediterranean Spirituality*, edited by A. H. Armstong.

Sams, Jamie, and David Carson. *Medicine Cards: The Discovery of Power Through the Ways of Animals*. Illustrated by Angela C. Werneke. Santa Fe, NM: Bear & Company, 1988.

Scully, Vincent. *The Earth, the Temple, and the Gods: Greek Sacred Architecture*. New York: Frederick A. Praeger, 1969.

Seike, Kiyoshi, Masanobyu Kudo, and David H. Engel, *A Japanese Touch for Your Garden*. Tokyo and New York: Kodansha International, 1992.

Spear, William. *Feng Shui Made Easy: Designing Your Life with the Ancient Art of Placement*. San Francisco: HarperSanFrancisco, 1995.

Spence, Lewis. *Ancient Egyptian Myths and Legends*. Reprint. New York: Dover Publications, 1990.

Stadelmann, Peter. *Water Gardens*. New York: Barron's, Hauppage, 1992.

Steiger, Brad. *Totems: The Transformative Power of Your Personal Animal Totem*. San Francisco: HarperSanFrancisco, 1997.

Stone, Merlin. *Ancient Mirrors of Womanhood: A Treasury of Goddess and Heroine Lore from Around the World*. Boston: Beacon Press, 1990.

————. *When God Was a Woman*. New York: Harcourt, Brace, Jovanovich, 1976.

Streep, Peg, ed. *The Sacred Journey: Prayers and Songs of Native America*. Illustrated by Claudia Karabic Sargent. Boston: Bulfinch Press, 1995.

Tagore, Rabindranath. *Stray Birds*. New York: The Macmillian Company, 1916.

Thomas, David Hurst, Jay Miller, Richard White, Peter Nabokov, and Philip J. Deloria. *The Native Americans*. Atlanta: Turner Publishing, 1993.

Thomas, William, and Kate Pavitt. *The Book of Talismans, Amulets, and Zodiacal Gems*. Reprint of 1914 edition. Kila, MT: Kessinger Publishing Company, n.d.

Tomocik, Joseph, with Leslie Garisto. *Water Gardening*. New York: Pantheon Books, 1996.

von Cles-Redon, Sibylle. *The Realm of the Great Goddess: The Story of the Megalith Builders*. Translated by Eric Mosbacher. Engelwood Cliffs, NJ: Prentice-Hall, 1962.

Waddell, L. Austine. *Tibetan Buddhism: With Its Mystic Cults, Symbolism, and Mythology*. Reprint. New York: Dover Publications, 1972.

Walker, Barbara F. *The Book of Sacred Stones: Facts and Fallacy in the Crystal World*. San Francisco: HarperSanFrancisco, 1989.

———. *The Woman's Dictionary of Symbols and Sacred Objects*. San Francisco, Harper & Row, 1988.

———. *The Woman's Encyclopedia of Myth and Secrets*. San Francisco, Harper & Row, 1983.

Williams, C. A. S. *Outlines of Chinese Symbolism and Art Motives*. Reprint. New York: Dover Publications, 1976.

Acknowledgments

Many people were kind enough to share their altar-building experiences with me during the course of writing this book; I discovered, among other things, that people who create sacred space are very nice! Each of them chose how to be identified in the text, and a few chose to remain anonymous. A very heartfelt thank-you to everyone, named or unnamed, and most particularly to those who sent me photographs of their altars or who allowed me to tromp through their sacred space, camera in hand. Blessings to all, listed here in alphabetical order: Gerard Bizzaro; Nancy Blair, writer and artist and proprietor of the Great Goddess Collection, a source of beautiful things; Frank Boros, helpful and kind; Ann Evans, a dedicated ritualist with wonderful ideas; Diane Garisto, whose spirit shines in her voice; Leslie Garisto for moral support and particularly for her gardening expertise; Marilyn Goldman, proprietor of Sidedoor Press and Altar Your Life, who has been a great help and who sells wonderful altars; Martha Trachtenberg Griffith; Tom Griffith; Donna Howell-Sickles, who helped me see the cowgirl in all women; Peter Israel for various and sundry good deeds, and much more, which only he knows about; Jane Lahr for friendship; Ed Mickens for being the West Coast Connection and a good friend; Julie (Jess) Middleton for all of her enthusiasm and expertise, particularly on songs and music, and for sharing her words with me; Clotilde Crawford Mifsad, of Goddess Tours to Malta; Cindy Pavlinac, a great photographer who builds wonderful altars and who is always there when I ask; Lyda Perrier; Lily Pfaff, an altar builder in the making; Claudia Karabaic Sargent for everything we've shared, including the wonderful illustrations in this book; Mrs. Justine Scott; Lori Stein for her help on Oriental gardens and Judaica; Oralee Stiles, spiritual director and altar builder; Sarah Teofanov, community ritualist and artist, whose artwork and altars are an inspiration; and Rob Ward.

Thanks, too, are due to Anne Edelstein, to Lisa Bach, to Caroline Pincus who saw the book through and then some, and to Terri Leonard and Martha Blegen.

And, of course and as always, to the best child in the world—you know who you are.

Index

Page numbers of illustrations appear in italics

frog, 62, 130
fruits. *See also specific fruits*
    on altar, offerings, 160–64

Gaia/Ge, earth herself, 51
gammadian symbol, 65
Ganesh, Indian elephant god, 11, 51,
    129, *159*
garlic, 155
garnet, 110, 112
gemstones, for altars, 11, 107–17. *See*
    also specific stones
  Medieval church, 81
geometric shapes, for altars. *See* shapes
God, Christian, symbols, 64. *See also*
    Christ; Christian symbols;
    Judeo-Christian
goddesses. *See specific goddesses*
gold, 44, 108, 112
gong, 101, 104
goose, 130
Gordian Knot, 70
Grace Cathedral, 181
grain, 141–42
gray color, 46
Great Mother (Magna Mater),
    symbols of, 35, 80, 121, 144.
    See also Cybele
Greece, ancient. *See also specific*
    gods/goddesses
  amber, 109
  amulets, 35
  animals and gods/goddesses, 118,
    119, 122–36
  ash tree, 149
  conch shell, 167
  cymbals, 103
  cypress tree, 150
  Fates, or Moirae, 40, 69, 150

Graces, 48
grain in, 142
hermae, 177
household worship, 5
incense, 94
jars/*amphorae*, 60
malachite, 114
myrtle tree, 151
number symbolism, 78, 81–82
oak tree, 151
offerings, 139–47
palm tree, 152
pinecone symbol, 152
poplar tree, 152
rites in, 4
and thyme, 157
weaving of *peplos*, 40
and white, 43
willow tree, 153
yew tree, 153
green color, 14, 23, 26, 44, 45, 46, 91,
    97

halo, 92
hand symbol, 61, 67–68
Hapi, Egyptian goddess, 44
Hathor, Egyptian goddess of the cos-
    mos, 51, 69, 101, 118, 124, 148,
    152
hearth, as holy place, 4
Hecate, triple goddess of fertility and
    crossroads of life, 51–52, 124,
    178
  garden for, 191–92
  and garlic, 155
  and key, 68
  and rose, 165
  Supper of, 139
  and three as symbolic number, 80